FOUNDATIONS

FOUNDATIONS

100 DAYS OF DEVOTIONS
THROUGH CATECHISM

Matthew Crocker

WIPF & STOCK · Eugene, Oregon

FOUNDATIONS
100 Days of Devotions through Catechism

Wipf & Stock
An Imprint of Wipf and Stock Publishers
199 W. 8th Ave., Suite 3
Eugene, OR 97401

www.wipfandstock.com

PAPERBACK ISBN: 978-1-6667-1487-6
HARDCOVER ISBN: 978-1-6667-1488-3
EBOOK ISBN: 978-1-6667-1489-0

AUGUST 13, 2021

This book is dedicated to my beautiful wife, Jodie. Her encouragement and unfounded love have helped carry me through this project.

It is also dedicated to my son, Hudson. "I wish you alone of all people in the world would do better than me in all things." (Cicero)

Contents

Acknowledgments

I WOULD FIRST LIKE to thank my wife for the patient endurance she showed while I was working on this project. I would also like to thank my close friends, Jon Bryars and Gareth Clegg, who encouraged me to pursue publishing and supported me as true friends in the faith. Likewise, thank you to Ross Hastings, who connected me with the team at Wipf & Stock. I would also like to thank my family. Finally, I would like to thank my church community at Christ City. I am so thankful for the continual encouragement, support, and prayers. In particular, I would like to thank Brett Landry, Jake LeFave, and Brandt Van Roekel for the willingness to help me in a multitude of ways during this endeavor.

Introduction

Why Read This Book?

IT IS BECOMING INCREASINGLY apparent that the Western world is growing ever more hostile towards the church of Jesus Christ. While this reality was to be expected—as Christ himself teaches, "Blessed are you when people hate you, when they exclude you and insult you and reject your name as evil, because of the Son of Man" (Luke 6:22)—our inability to reconcile with this fact was unexpected. It appears that, rather than accept the persecutions that we seem to face (minor in comparison to other churches around the world), the Western church has struggled to wrestle with this. The reason for this is simple; biblical and theological illiteracy. Our own inability to rest in Scriptural truth and theological statements of faith has led to a degeneracy within the church that prioritizes manners over morals and niceness over Christlikeness.

This state of affairs is not the fault of outside forces consistently lambasting the church, but it's our fault—the very people in the pews. Somewhere along the way we as a church decided that the metric of success was not faithfulness but impact. Therefore, the boundaries for membership, access to communion, baptism, and other entry markers were reduced to the point where the church became a place for religious refugees looking for a way to feel good, but not a home for pilgrims on their way to heaven. Our desire to see the church grow led us to create a church that has standards so low that in some cases you don't even need to fully articulate the gospel in order to become a member.

Historically this has not been the case. The expectations on church membership, baptism, and the Lord's supper were quite high. People were expected to memorize confessions, creeds, the ten commandments, as well as passages like the Lord's prayer. We need to realize that the biblical and theological illiteracy of our day is not a result of cultural decline but a result of bad ecclesiology. None of this is to suggest that there are not churches working very hard to see biblical literacy rates rise among their congregations and the people in their cities. No one can deny that there are many churches which faithfully proclaim the gospel and want their congregants to know the gospel. I am merely pointing out a cultural trend I have noticed as a member of evangelical Protestantism.

Luckily there is a potential antidote to the problem we are currently facing. A return to confessionally orthodox beliefs that build up biblical and theological literacy. Donald Bloesch in his book *The Church* writes, "The need today is neither for a therapeutic church nor for a political church but for a confessing church, one that will boldly confess the claims of Christ in the face of the heresies and heterodoxies of our age."[1] We do not need more churches that attempt to make us feel good about ourselves. Nor do we need more churches that earnestly strive to involve themselves in politics to win a particular crowd. We need a church that is willing to confess, in all honesty, the gospel of Jesus Christ and what that entails for daily life. This needs to be done with candor and integrity even where that becomes uncomfortable. It needs to be done with rigor so that our congregations know the beliefs of the church. But also, it needs to be done in genuine love and with a genuine desire to see people personally united to Jesus Christ. Love for God will drive us to love those around us and growing in our biblical and theological literacy will help us to share this love with others.

It is true that we live in a time of growing discord, but it is my belief that as we reclaim biblical and theological literacy we can love the world in a more concrete way. The world will always seek to destroy the church, but the church has the opportunity in that destruction to show the self-sacrificing love of God. Dietrich Bonhoeffer was well acquainted with a church of lackadaisical faith and a world that hated Christian love. He writes, "This world is engaged in a life-and-death struggle with the church-community. Still, it is the task and the essence of the church-community to proclaim precisely to this world its reconciliation with God, and to disclose to it the reality of the love of God, against which the world so blindly rages."[2] If we are going to proclaim the kind of reconciliation Bonhoeffer advocates then we need to know the basics: why do we need reconciliation, what do we

1. Bloesch, *Church*, 34.
2. Bonhoeffer, *Ethics*, 17.

need reconciliation to, who is God, who is Jesus, and more. This will come as we recommit to raising our biblical and theological literacy.

What is this book?

This book is an attempt to provide some semblance of a solution to the problem outlined above. It is an attempt to synthesize biblical and theological reflection into one short work that can be utilized to learn the foundations of Christian belief. Whether or not this task has been accomplished will be up to you to decide for yourself. What you will find within this work is something you may or may not be familiar with; *The Westminster Shorter Catechism*. Catechism is a summary of Christian beliefs using a question-and-answer format for the purposes of teaching. Catechesis is a Greek word meaning "instruction by word of mouth" and has long been a tradition that the church has utilized to help its members learn the foundational elements of Christian belief. Kenda Creasy Dean writes this about the practice of catechism, "Catechesis clarifies the church's understanding of who God is; shapes our ability to participate in the Christian community; provides the means for discerning our call as disciples and for claiming our hope in God's future."[3] In other words catechesis—instruction—is the way in which we learn to follow Jesus.

Due to changing cultural norms the language of *The Westminster Shorter Catechism* has been updated in order to make it more readable for a twenty-first century audience while maintaining the doctrinal truths found within. Likewise, some revisions have been made so that it could reflect the church tradition I am a part of, the Anabaptist. To readers familiar with *The Westminster Shorter Catechism*, you may feel as if the updates are so extensive you do not even recognize it; that is okay. As long as this work is useful in helping people grow in their knowledge of truth I do not really mind if its revisions bother some readers. This book's structure is designed to allow for immersion in God's Word, reflection on theological topics, and prayer. Each question-and-answer has a brief Scripture passage associated with it, a reflection on the theological topic, questions to ponder, and a written prayer.

Catechesis, the intentional instruction of people in God's Word, is an extremely important task that we cannot afford to defer responsibility on.

3. Dean, *Almost Christian*, 63.

The task at hand is not primarily for full-time or part-time ministers of God's word but it is for everyone. We as a church have a responsibility to offer our services in discipling the young Christians in our midst. Parents need to model the love of Christ in the home, but they also need to teach their children the essentials of Christianity. Older congregants need to share the years of wisdom and experience they have from walking with Christ to those they encounter on a regular basis. This task is not simply a one-and-done affair but is an all-of-life twenty-four-seven reality that extends to every area of our lives. We either adopt the spirit of catechesis or we are disobedient to Christ's command to "make disciples" (Matt 28:19). The quicker we recognize that we all are in desperate need of growth in our knowledge about God the quicker we will begin the task of studying God's word—of catechizing ourselves—to know him more. None of us are ever too old, too mature, to participate in catechesis. As Wilhelmus à Brakel, a Dutch theologian from the seventeenth century, reminds us, "The word of God is necessary and profitable not only for beginners and little ones but also for the most advanced and spiritual believers here upon earth. It is a brook from which a lamb may drink and an ocean in which an elephant can drown."[4]

All of us are in desperate need for more of God's word in our life. Catechesis instructs us in that word and grows us in our love for Jesus. It is time to leave the feel-good church behind because it does not feel so good anymore. It's a cheap impersonation of Christ's bride and we are beginning to wake up to the reality that the tent pegs of doctrine have been moved so far that the bride of Christ we used to be a part of is no longer what we thought it was. We are like Jacob awakening after his wedding night with Rachel but "there was Leah" (Gen 29:25)! Yet, let this not be cause for alarm. The gospel of Jesus Christ has the power to transform and it is as we commit ourselves to God, repent of our sin, and turn to proper instruction in the word that his Spirit will fill and renew us. While we are unable to manipulate God towards revival, I do not doubt that "God often ties his decision to the persevering prayers of the faithful and the diligent study of his Word. If the church begins to reform itself in light of God's Word, the strong possibility is that revival will not be far away."[5]

4. Brakel, *The Christian's Reasonable Service*, 73.
5. Bloesch, *The Church*, 188.

How do I use this book?

This answer is multifaceted as this book is designed to be used in a multitude of ways. Its primary purpose is to be used as a personal devotional book. The decision on how to do this is obviously left up to you, but I have some suggestions for how you can use this book for growth in relationship and knowledge of God.

I would suggest going through one question-and-answer per day taking time to read it, re-read it, and read it again to internalize the truth of the answer through memorization. You can then reflect upon the passage of Scripture, slowly reading and reflecting upon what the Holy Spirit is saying to you through the text. Then read the reflection slowly and examine your heart in relation to what has just been read. The personal reflection questions can be utilized in this process as well to help you think upon the reflection. Finish off this personal devotion time by reading and praying through the prayer provided. Treat this prayer as a suggestion on what to pray for not as an exhaustive prayer on the topic. Obviously, praying beyond the provided prayer is encouraged.

Of course, this is not the only way this book can be utilized. It can also be used in a small group where memorization of the question-and-answer, reading the Scripture and reflection, and prayer take place on one's own and then are discussed in a small group setting. My guess is that catechism in community would only help you to internalize these truths even more. Likewise, this book can be used very effectively as a family discipleship tool. In fact, this would be my ultimate desire for this book; that it is a useful tool in helping parents reclaim the spiritual formation of their children. A father or mother could read and reflect upon the question-and-answer, Scripture, and reflection and then bring what they have learnt to their children. The memorization of the question-and-answer could be expected of the children and discussion could ensue about what it means. As parents it's important to note that we have consistently been shown to have an exponentially greater impact on the faith of our children than anyone else. It is our initiative in learning ourselves that will demonstrate the value of learning to our children. Kenda Dean Creasy demonstrates this well when she writes,

> Parents are not called to make their children godly . . . The law
> called upon Jewish parents to show their children godliness – to
> teach them, talk to them, embody for them their own delight in

the Lord 24/7. Everything they needed for their children's faith formation; God had already given them. In the end, awakening faith does not depend on how hard we press young people to love God, but on how much we show them that we do.[6]

Finally, this book can also be used effectively as a curriculum within a youth ministry or kid's ministry if the content is effectively communicated at the level of children involved. In fact, this book is the result of two years of experimentation with teaching this catechism at the Youth Ministry in which I work. The question-and-answer can be read aloud together and memorized, the teacher can lead students through a discussion based on the question-and-answer and the Scripture reading, and the catechism can be provided as a resource for parents to help them talk with their kids about what they are learning. This is an excellent way to partner with parents in the discipleship of their children.

Clearly this book can be utilized in several different ways. And the reason that I so keenly outline the different ways it can be used is because I truly believe that the intentional discipleship of people in Scripture and theology will form them to be resilient followers of Jesus. I believe that if we reclaim the art of catechesis, if we desire to know God in a deeper way, if we commit to reading Scripture, prayerfully meditating upon it and the truths therein, that God will do a mighty work by his Holy Spirit. Praise be to God.

6. Dean, *Almost Christian*, 120.

DAY 1

Q. What is a person's purpose in life?

**A. A person's purpose in life is to glorify God
and enjoy him forever.**

*For you are great and do marvelous deeds; you alone are God. Teach
me your way, Lord, that I may rely on your faithfulness; give me an
undivided heart, that I may fear your name. I will praise you, Lord my
God, with all my heart; I will glorify your name forever.*

—PSALM 86:10-12

IN OUR WORLD, PURPOSE is often thought of in terms of careers, goals,
dreams, and things that we look to for a fulfilling life. It can be argued,
therefore, that much of our anxiety in life is the result of the dissonance
between chasing our *purpose* and the lack of fulfillment we receive when we
achieve or attain that thing we desired so much. The sad result of this chase
is proof that these things were never meant to be a person's purpose in life.

Careers, goals, and dreams are fleeting and prone to change from day
to day. They can be taken away from us in a moment, whether we like to
admit this or not. Unforeseen circumstances might arise which strip these
things from us. Life situations might impede the fulfillment of our dream
job or career goal. Instead of building our purpose upon these vaporous
things we need a purpose that is a foundation. We need a purpose that
provides a firm foundation for us to build our whole lives upon. If purpose
can be radically shifted as our external circumstances change, then we are
left without any real stable foundation at all. Instead of aiming towards a

1

purpose which we find fulfilling, we end up unsettled and anxious as the false purposes we build upon crumble beneath us.

Therefore, our purpose must be sure. It needs to be unchanging and everlasting. It needs to be given to us, bestowed upon us, from an unchangeable outside source. As long as our purpose is tied to this world, as long as it is changeable, we will be unhappy. But when our purpose is sure, when it is unchangeable, regardless of the circumstances we find ourselves in, we find joy.

Hence, our answer argues that we receive purpose from God. God actually created us with a purpose in mind and it's his purpose for us that is our purpose in life. Our purpose is that we build our lives upon him as the one who sustains us. It's that we seek to honor him as our Creator and worship him for all eternity. It's that we look to him as God alone. And in this we also enjoy God as the source of all that is good in the world. It's as we glorify him by giving him praise and honor in our prayers, worship, and daily life that all his good provisions are brought before our minds and we begin to find our greatest joy in him. In other words, God has created us for two things: 1) To give him glory, and 2) to enjoy him completely.

Reflection Questions

1. What does it mean to glorify God?

2. When you think of the purpose of your life, what comes to mind?

Prayer

Lord, would you help me to live into your purpose for me? Would you begin to work in my life to worship you and to enjoy you? Help me to turn away from the vain purposes of the world and look to you for purpose. Strengthen me to honor you with my whole life. I pray that you would allow me to do this all my days. Amen.

DAY 2

Q. What has God given to show us how we glorify
and enjoy him?

A. The Bible shows us how we glorify and enjoy him.

*But as for you, continue in what you have learned and have become
convinced of, because you know those from whom you learned it, and
how from infancy you have known the holy Scriptures, which are able
to make you wise for salvation through faith in Christ Jesus. All Scripture is God-breathed and is useful for teaching, rebuking, correcting and
training in righteousness, so that the servant of God may be thoroughly
equipped for every good work.*

—2 TIMOTHY 3:14-17

ONE OF THE MOST precious gifts we have is God's word in the Bible.
Unfortunately, we often take this wonderful treasure for granted. Perhaps
this is due to an abundance of availability. In previous generations, access
to the Bible was restricted to those who had the means to afford books
and had the ability to read them. However, nowadays anyone can access
Scripture in numerous formats, from audio Bibles to mobile applications.

Theoretically we would expect a zealous desire for interaction with
God's word to come with such an abundance of access to it, but this has not
been the case. The sinfulness of the human heart prevents us from taking
God's word seriously. In our sin we tend to mischaracterize the Bible as
rules or antiquated tales of fictional people doing fictional things. We com-
partmentalize Scripture as myth and, therefore, ignore its value. Yet, this

3

amazing book is not primarily a list of rules or a collection of nice bedtime stories, but it is the grand story of the entire universe.

The Bible is the story of God's interaction with humanity throughout history. It is the story of God's good creation of everything, man's subsequent fall into sin bringing about serious calamity for the world, and God working to restore us into right relationship with him and other people. It's the grand narrative of cosmic reconciliation culminating in the Living Word, Jesus Christ, the Great Redeemer of the universe. This was not an afterthought. God, in his infinite wisdom, ordained it from eternity past that Jesus, his own Son, would be the source of this redemption. It was Jesus who made it possible for us to glorify God and enjoy him through his vicarious atonement of our sins on the cross. It is through Jesus and by Jesus—as we come to him in the written word of the Bible—that we can glorify God and enjoy him forever.

Reflection Questions

1. How often do you read the Bible?
2. Do you think of Jesus as the focal point of the whole Bible?

Prayer

Lord, show us your son Jesus in the Bible. I pray that you would help us to read your word more. Help us to see its value and goodness in our lives. Father, we confess that we do not go to your word enough. We ask that you, by your Holy Spirit, would kindle a desire for your word in our hearts and fan it into flame. Amen.

DAY 3

Q. What does the Bible teach us?

A. The Bible teaches us what we believe about God
and what God requires of us.

*The law of the Lord is perfect, refreshing the soul. The statutes of the
Lord are trustworthy, making wise the simple. The precepts of the Lord
are right, giving joy to the heart. The commands of the Lord are radiant,
giving light to the eyes. The fear of the Lord is pure, enduring forever. The
decrees of the Lord are firm, and all of them are righteous.*

—PSALM 19:7–9

As WE READ OUR Bibles, we begin to see the beauty of the story God has
embedded within history. It's as we follow along with the narrative of how
God acts toward his people that we begin to understand more about who
God is. We see that God is good, that God is gracious, that God is loving,
and that God is merciful from the first pages to the last pages of the Bible.
But we also see that God is perfectly just, wrathful, and holy. So much so
that sin and evil can't coexist with this God. In Scripture we come face to
face with the God of grace who judges sin in his perfect righteousness. And
all of these things that we learn about God are on full display in the person
and work of Jesus Christ.

Jesus shows us God's love and goodness by going to the cross for our
sins: "But God demonstrates his own love for us in this: While we were
still sinners, Christ died for us" (Rom 5:8). Jesus shows us God's justice
and holiness by taking the punishment for sin upon himself: "God made
him who had no sin to be sin for us, so that in him we might become the

righteousness of God" (2 Cor 5:21). And Jesus shows us what is required of God's people now that they have been reconciled to God: "Jesus replied: 'Love the Lord your God with all your heart and with all your soul and with all your mind.' This is the first and greatest commandment. And the second is like it: 'Love your neighbor as yourself'" (Matt 22:37–39). It is only in the Bible that these glorious realities are revealed to us and that is why we cherish this book above all others.

Yet apart from God working in our hearts as we read his word, we are unable to fully understand the realities presented to us in it. In our sinfulness we are utterly incapable of reasoning our way up to God. Our armchair theology may sometimes produce results partially in line with the God of the Bible, but it will always fall short of his self-revelation to us, meaning that it will always distort God's character. Instead, we need God himself, in the person of the Holy Spirit, and through his word, to reveal himself to us and open our eyes so that we can understand Scripture. Just as a person cannot see in the dark without light, we cannot understand the Scriptures in a saving way apart from God's illuminating light in our lives. This is a light that only comes through the power of the Holy Spirit working in our hearts.

Reflection Questions

1. What is your favorite Bible story?
2. How important is the Bible in your daily life?

Prayer

Heavenly Father, we pray that you would help us see you in the Bible. Help us turn to your word more than we already do and reveal yourself to us as we read. Lord, we pray that your Holy Spirit would show us how the whole Bible points to your Son, Jesus Christ. We ask that we might know Jesus more and that we might see him on every page of this amazing book. Amen.

Day 4

Q. What is God?

A. God is the being who created everything.

Praise the Lord, my soul. Lord my God, you are very great; you are clothed with splendor and majesty. The Lord wraps himself in light as with a garment; he stretches out the heavens like a tent and lays the beams of his upper chambers on their waters.

—PSALM 104:1–3

WE ARE INTRODUCED TO God in the Bible as Creator. Before anything else existed in the universe, God was. And it was by his word that God created everything that exists. He spoke all things into existence, including mountains, animal, plants, and human beings. The breath of his mouth brought life to everything in creation. For this reason, we are completely subordinate to God, completely under his authority. He is the Creator and we are his creatures. When we create it is secondary, it is always made of other stuff. When he created it was primary, it was made from nothing. As Creator he "has put everything under his feet" and he rules over the creation (1 Cor 15:27). This idea is of fundamental importance to Christianity. The reason we submit to God is not because of his goodness, mercy, grace, or any other reason beneficial to us. This would make submission to God contingent upon something else. Rather, submission to God is predicated upon God's lordship and the fact the he is our Creator. It is a submission grounded in who he is, not what he does.

Likewise, the reality that God has created us and everything around us imbues creation with importance and value. Unlike the view of the world which sees creation as a chance happenstance that we can utilize as a means to our own ends, Christians recognize creation as inherently valuable because it was made by an infinitely valuable God. It's only as we reflect on the fact that God is Creator that we will see creation as worthy of protection and care.

The idea of God as Creator is the seed from which the doctrines of his omnipotence (the doctrine that God is all powerful), his sovereignty (the doctrine that God is in charge), his omniscience (the doctrine that God knows all things), and others spring. In creation God's greatness is on full display and because of this it reveals our inability to offer him the praise he rightly deserves. Thus, we are left in a hopeless predicament. God the Creator demands our praise, but our praise is wildly inadequate. It has been irrevocably stained with the scourge of sin. But the very God who created the universe through his word also sent the living Word, Jesus Christ, into the world so that we might be reconciled to him as Creator. Through Jesus' death and resurrection, a way has been made for us to acknowledge our Creator God and worship him with our whole heart, mind, and strength.

Reflection Questions

1. What do you picture when you think of God creating everything?
2. Does knowing that God created you change the way you live?

Prayer

Holy Creator God, heavenly Father, we worship you as the one who brought everything into existence. Thank you for this good creation. Thank you for its beauty. Thank you for its intricacies. Lord, forgive us for not recognizing your eternal power and divine nature in your creation. We pray that you would help us to recognize that you are the Creator and we are the creatures. Amen.

Day 5

Q. Are there more gods than one?
A. There is only one God.

Hear, O Israel: The Lord our God, the Lord is one. Love the Lord your God with all your heart and with all your soul and with all your strength.

—DEUTERONOMY 6:4-5

THROUGHOUT HISTORY COUNTLESS RELIGIONS have come and gone that followed many different gods. In fact, in the course of human history it's only been recently that monotheism—the worship of one god—has become a more regular occurrence. The belief in many gods has always been the default position. Yet, the idea that there are a multitude of gods in the heavens presents us with insurmountable difficulties in understanding the world around us.

If there are more gods than one it becomes impossible to rely upon any of them. It is simply impossible to have more than one all-powerful being. Either one will be all-powerful and the others will not be God (in the true sense of that word), or neither will be all-powerful, meaning that their plans could be thwarted whenever the other wanted to stop them. This is self-evidently problematic to the very idea of God. God must be *one* or he can't be all-powerful. God must be *one* or he can't be all-knowing. God must be *one* or it's impossible to say that he's won.

Thankfully, God is one and so he is all-powerful, meaning he has the power to create with no impediment whatsoever. The power to destroy and nothing can prevent him from doing so. The power to forgive and nothing can deter him from offering this gift of grace. God's oneness means that he is absolutely and totally in charge. This is exactly what we see revealed in the Bible. God completely unhindered in the things he chooses to do.

One of the things God chooses to do, in Jesus Christ, is go to the cross and die for the forgiveness of sins. No power in the universe could have prevented him from accomplishing this plan of redemption. When we reflect upon this, we also realize that if this is true, then nothing can pluck us from his hand once we have been forgiven our sins. Nothing can separate us from the love of the all-powerful God. This is what Paul writes about in Romans where he says, "Who shall separate us from the love of Christ? Shall tribulation, or distress, or persecution, or famine, or nakedness, or danger, or sword? . . . No, in all these things we are more than conquerors through him who loved us" (Rom 8:35,37). In God's oneness—his oneness of being and his oneness of purpose—we have a firm foundation upon which to place our hope for the future.

Reflection Questions

1. What does God's oneness have to do with our hope for salvation?

2. How does knowing that God is "one" change the way you see his relationship with you?

Prayer

Gracious God, you are the all-powerful Creator of the universe. Your plans can't be stopped, and this is our hope. Everything you set out to accomplish happens. Nothing falls outside of your view. You alone have the power to save and you have planned that this would take place through your son Jesus. Thank you for saving us through his death and thank you for giving us new life through his resurrection.

DAY 6

Q. How many persons are in the godhead?

**A. There are three persons in the Godhead:
Father, Son, and Holy Spirit.**

*Then Jesus came to them and said, "All authority in heaven and on earth
has been given to me. Therefore go and make disciples of all nations,
baptizing them in the name of the Father and of the Son and of the Holy
Spirit, and teaching them to obey everything I have commanded you.
And surely I am with you always, to the very end of the age."*

—MATTHEW 28:18-20

IN THEOLOGY, "TRINITY" IS the word that we use to describe God's three-
ness in persons and oneness as God. So the Trinity is the direct focus of
the question-and-answer above. Here it is important to note that the word
"Trinity" is not actually found anywhere in the Bible. However, as God reveals himself throughout the biblical story, we encounter the concept of the
Trinity by seeing God designated as three persons: Father, Son, and Holy
Spirit. These names do not simply describe the different ways that different
authors within the Bible conceive of God. Rather, each of these designa-
tions refers to a distinct person within the Godhead, and yet to the one God
of the Bible. For this reason, Christians speak of God as existing in Trinity.
He is one God and three persons simultaneously.

Each of these persons is fully God. We must not see the persons of the
Trinity as parts in a larger whole, like a three-sectioned pie chart. Rather,
the Father is fully God, the Son is fully God, and the Holy Spirit is fully
God. But the Father is not the Son, and the Son is not the Holy Spirit, and

the Holy Spirit is not the Father. Traditionally, this is how the Trinity has been elaborated for believers of the Christian faith. God is one in three persons. This has huge implications for us. When Jesus, God's Son, died for our sins, it was God in his fullness who died for us. When we are indwelt by the Holy Spirit it is God in his fullness who dwells within us, giving us new life and new affections as we walk with him. When we address the Father in our prayers, we are addressing God in his entirety, not a portion of him.

This explanation of God may appear confusing and it is certainly not easy to understand. In fact, in many ways a full comprehension of how God is one in essence and three in persons is impossible for our feeble reason to comprehend. However, as we go to the Bible, we find that this reality is testified to repeatedly. Therefore, we do not seek to explain the mysterious way in which this works, we do not attempt to climb up to God with our mind, but we accept the testimony he makes about himself in Scripture. We accept who God is as he has revealed himself to us in his word so that we might understand.

Reflections Questions

1. Do you find the Trinity confusing?
2. How does it change the way you think about God to know he exists as Trinity?

Prayer

Our Father in heaven, thank you for revealing your Son Jesus to us through his birth. Lord, thank you for revealing your great love for us by dying for our sins. Thank you for sending the Holy Spirit to dwell within us when we believe in the gospel. We pray that we might reflect on the Trinity as we go to your word. We pray that we might learn to know you as you have revealed yourself to us. Amen.

DAY 7

Q. What are the decrees of God?

**A. The decrees of God are the eternal plans
that he has guaranteed to take place for his glory.**

Remember the former things, those of long ago; I am God, and there is no other; I am God, and there is none like me. I make known the end from the beginning, from ancient times, what is still to come. I say, "My purpose will stand, and I will do all that I please." From the east I summon a bird of prey; from a far-off land, a man to fulfill my purpose. What I have said, that I will bring about; what I have planned, that I will do.

—ISAIAH 46:9-11

SOMETIMES WE APPROACH EVENTS in this world as if God acts willy-nilly, almost as if he is as surprised by world events as we are. However, if this were the case then certainly our hope in the gospel would be lost. How could we trust that God's plans will be completed if he could be blindsided by world events?

How wonderful it is that this is not the God we believe in. The God of the Bible is a God who not only knows all things, but has purposed all things to take place. He is not merely an all-powerful observer of the universe, but he is the All-knowing Architect of history. God, before the foundation of the world, decreed every world event so that his perfect plan of redemption might be accomplished. He is the Great King who issues a decree encompassing all of existence. He has no need for the news because he receives no *new* information. He has orchestrated everything. God has made the universe in such a way that everything that happens comes about as a result of his will.

It is because of this that we can trust that God is working "all things" together for the good of "those who are called according to his purpose" (Rom 8:28). Even in our suffering we can trust that God has orchestrated our circumstances in such a way that the end result is for our benefit. Likewise, because of his decrees, we as Christians can know our salvation is secure. God as Trinity purposed, before the creation of the universe, that the Son would die for humanity's sins. God purposed it that the Holy Spirit would be sent to indwell those who believe in this great story of redemption. God purposed it that you and I would be saved through faith in him.

His will is not willy-nilly, it is not malevolent, and it is not capriciously against us. His will, based on the testimony of holy Scripture, is loving, kind, and gracious. He is disposed to favor us, to shower us with blessings. This is why we can be certain that our salvation is secure, because the God who rules the universe—the God who is never caught off guard—made it that way, and nothing can hold back his loving hand.

Reflection Questions

1. What do you find hard about God ruling over everything?
2. What encourages you about knowing that God rules over everything?

Prayer

All-powerful Father, help us to see you as the God who rules over everything in the universe. You know all things and you have ordained all things for your glory. Lord, we know that all things work together for our good. We pray that you would help us see this in new ways today. Amen.

DAY 8

Q. How does God accomplish his decrees?

A. God accomplishes his decrees through creation and providence.

Ah, Sovereign Lord, you have made the heavens and the earth by your great power and outstretched arm. Nothing is too hard for you. You show love to thousands but bring the punishment for the parents' sins into the laps of their children after them. Great and mighty God, whose name is the Lord Almighty, great are your purposes and mighty are your deeds. Your eyes are open to the ways of all mankind; you reward each person according to their conduct and as their deeds deserve.

—JEREMIAH 32:17–19

ONE OF HUMANITY'S WEAKNESSES is that it can't complete the things it sets out to do. Sometimes we make amazing progress in various areas—such as engineering, medicine, or physics—but in many other ways we tend to fail in our accomplishments. On the one hand, it doesn't take a genius to recognize the marvel of human accomplishment. Simply look at the cityscapes that dot the entirety of the earth. From major metropolises to silicone microchips in iPhones, we know that humans can accomplish great things. But on the other hand, it is also glaringly obvious where we fail to achieve the things we originally purpose to do. We see unfinished road works, failures of technology, and more that show us we don't always finish what we set out to finish.

We see this in our personal lives as well. We are all familiar with the feeling of setting out to accomplish a task and yet being completely unable

15

to finish the job. We try to fix something in our home, but a few hours later we call the plumber. We try to buckle down and get our schoolwork done, but a few minutes later we are playing video games. We try to set a goal for New Year's, and within a month we've given up. Procrastination, distraction, and a lack of perseverance might just be one of the most common human experiences.

In this area we differ significantly from God. He does not wrestle with procrastination, distraction, or an inability to complete the task before him. Whatever God purposed before the foundation of the world he *will* accomplish. The All-powerful Creator of the universe would be inconsistent with his character if he were unable to accomplish his will. He would either be impotent and therefore not omnipotent, or incompetent and therefore not omniscient. Neither of these things are true of God. He is both potent and competent and, therefore, he accomplishes everything he sets out to accomplis. Full stop.

However, this still leaves open the question of how God accomplishes his decrees. Biblically speaking, the ways that God has chosen to accomplish everything he sets out to accomplish (his decrees), is through the work of creation and his work of providence. He made the universe so that his purposes could be fulfilled, and he filled the universe in such a way that he rules over it completely to his purposed end. These two works will be discussed further in the coming questions-and-answers but for now we can know that God uses these two things to complete what he sets out to accomplish and nothing prevents him from doing so.

Reflection Questions

1. Have you ever started something you couldn't finish?
2. What comes to your mind when you think of God never having to deal with this?

Prayer

Father, you are the All-powerful God of the universe whose plans are always accomplished. We take great comfort in knowing that nothing can prevent you from doing what you want to do. Lord, work in our hearts to show us how you rule over everything in your creation. Amen.

Day 9

Q. What is the work of creation?

A. The work of creation is God making everything out of nothing and declaring it good.

In the beginning God created the heavens and the earth. Now the earth was formless and empty, darkness was over the surface of the deep, and the Spirit of God was hovering over the waters. And God said, "Let there be light," and there was light. God saw that the light was good, and he separated the light from the darkness.

—GENESIS 1:1–4

IT'S AMAZING TO THINK that once upon a time none of what we see in the world existed. Before God began his creating work, nothing was here, nada. It's not as if God took some sort of material and formed the universe out of it. He did not mold the universe like a Play-Doh sculpture with some preexisting cosmos clay that he had lying around. It's not as if God saw a really messy universe, where everything already existed, and he just needed to give it order and clean it up a little bit. No, before God created there was nothing. Then God spoke and there was something. All it took was his word of power and the thing that we call the universe came into existence.

Obviously, this shows us God's power, we would never deny that. But it also shows us something of far greater significance—it shows us God's free grace. Before anything existed, God was completely perfect in himself. He needed absolutely nothing. He always and forever existed in perfection. He even had a perfect relationship within himself in the persons of the Trinity. He didn't need anything. Yet, despite this he chose to create everything. We didn't deserve to be created. It's not as if we are owed the things of this world. God simply created out of his love and goodness for no reason other than his own desire. The perfect God of the universe created us simply because he wanted to.

Not only was creation a work of God's grace, but creation was equally an act of God's loving-kindness. God did not have to create something people would find good. Yet God completed his creation and exclaimed that it was "very good" (Gen 1:31). He made things in such a way that the first people would enjoy it as paradise. Thus, creation points us toward praise. We should be thankful to God for creating us, we should recognize that he is all-powerful and worship him, and we should give him the glory because he is the God of grace.

Reflection Questions

1. Think about creation out of nothing. Is this something that is hard to understand?

2. Why did God create us?

Prayer

Creator of heaven and earth, we worship you and praise you for creating everything that exists. Lord, your word of power brought everything into existence from absolutely nothing. You did this out of your own goodness, not because we deserve it. Father, teach us by the Holy Spirit to honor you as the God of grace who gives because it is your desire. Amen.

DAY 10

Q. How did God create people?

A. God created people male and female in his image.

Then God said, "Let us make mankind in our image, in our likeness, so that they may rule over the fish in the sea and the birds in the sky, over the livestock and all the wild animals, and over all the creatures that move along the ground." So God created mankind in his own image, in the image of God he created them; male and female he created them. God blessed them and said to them, "Be fruitful and increase in number; fill the earth and subdue it. Rule over the fish in the sea and the birds in the sky and over every living creature that moves on the ground."

—GENESIS 1:26–28

WE SHOULDN'T SKIM OVER this biblical truth. It's easy to miss, but if we do miss it then we are going to be without one the great truths of Scripture, and we will struggle to see other people as valuable. This truth is that humankind was created in such a way that we reflect God himself. This is a great gift. God, in his perfection, chose to make human beings so that they resembled him. What this means we don't exactly know. It's pointless to enter debates about what the "image of God" means. What we do know is that it definitely is a sign that humanity has been honored above everything else that has been created. Even the angels are not said to be created in the image of God.

The implications of this are massive. Our world thinks we are special because we are all unique, but the Bible tells us we are special because we are all alike in the image of the Creator. Our world teaches us that we have inalienable human rights which cannot be trampled upon, but gives us no reason why we should have these rights. The doctrine of the image of God does. The world teaches us that who we are is defined by what we do, but the Bible tells us that who we are is defined by being his image-bearers. We are all created in his image—both man and woman—and therefore equal and valuable in the sight of God.

Here we need to realize, once again, that God did not have to create us this way. He created plenty of animals and creatures before humanity that were not made in his image. We didn't deserve to be created this way. We didn't deserve to be the pinnacle, the excellence, of God's creation, but God, in his gracious wisdom, made it so. Being image-bearers is, therefore, an act of God's grace. Unfortunately, sin has drastically marred this image and has caused us to boast in ourselves. Sin has caused us to look upon ourselves and see our greatness as something deserved, instead of seeing it as something bestowed upon us by God in his grace. It's true that we still retain certain aspects of God's image even in this fallen condition. But if we are to enjoy the full pleasures of being made in God's image, we need to confess our brokenness apart from God and recognize the ultimate bearer of God's image, Jesus Christ. It's as we humbly submit ourselves before the lordship of Christ that we are fully restored in the image of God.

Reflection Questions

1. What do you think of when you hear "image of God?"

2. Do you see God as a gift-giver and do you deserve those gifts?

Prayer

Father in heaven, we ask that you help us see how we are created to image you to the rest of the world. Lord, thank you for creating us this way. Thank you for giving us this amazing honor. We pray that you would strengthen us to live in your image every day. Amen.

Day 11

Q. What is God's work of providence?

A. God's work of providence is his care for and governing of all creatures.

Are not two sparrows sold for a penny? Yet not one of them will fall to the ground outside your Father's care. And even the very hairs of your head are all numbered. So don't be afraid; you are worth more than many sparrows.

—MATTHEW 10:29-31

GOD ACCOMPLISHES EVERYTHING HE sets out to accomplish through his work of creation and his work of providence. Most of us are probably not that familiar with the word "providence." It is an old theological word that people don't really use anymore in their daily conversations and thus, we need to define it. Providence is God's continual care for creation. It is God using his divine energy to carefully preserve everything that exists, including you and me. It is his moment-by-moment work of sustaining and maintaining every created thing; every cell, every movement of the planets; every subatomic particle which we haven't yet discovered.

This means that God did not simply create the universe, dust off his hands, and then relax in his La-Z-Boy on the seventh day. He didn't set up the universe as some perpetual motion machine that no longer requires divine power to continue forward. Instead, God continues to maintain all things—at all times—to such an extent that if he ever removed his care for his creation, it would simply cease to exist. As Paul says to the Athenians on Mars Hill, "For in him we live and move and have our being" (Acts 17:28).

In other words, everything, including all the things we do during our days, is because God sustains it and wills it.

Therefore, we must look at our lives and allow the doctrine of God's providence to soften our hearts to the grace of God that we see present in his powerful sustenance. Ask yourself these questions to stir up your heart to worship his mighty providential care: Have you ever wondered why you wake up safe and sound each morning? Have you ever wondered why you are alive at this point in history rather than at some other time? Have you ever wondered why you exist and not somebody else? Ponder these things and you will begin to see that God is under no obligation to see you through each night. That he was under no obligation to place you amidst your family or in this decade. That he was under no obligation to create you at all. And in this way God's gracious love becomes clearer to our sight. It is as we reflect upon this providential care and apply it to our lives that the veil of self-confidence clouding our vision is removed, allowing us to see clearly the gracious sustaining love of God. We call this gracious sustaining love God's work of providence.

Reflection Questions

1. What are some ways God is sustaining you right now?
2. How does this change your view of how much God cares for you?

Prayer

Gracious God, you care for us every minute of the day. You sustain us and lead us each and every day. Lord, would you give us eyes to see how much we rely on you? Help us understand how this is your grace towards us. Nothing we do earns your care. We worship you and praise you, God. Amen.

DAY 12

Q. What special act of providence did God show towards Adam and Eve when they were created?

A. When God created Adam and Eve he promised that he would dwell with them and that they would live forever if they were obedient.

Then the Lord God formed a man from the dust of the ground and breathed into his nostrils the breath of life, and the man became a living being. Now the Lord God had planted a garden in the east, in Eden; and there he put the man he had formed. The Lord God made all kinds of trees grow out of the ground—trees that were pleasing to the eye and good for food. In the middle of the garden were the tree of life and the tree of the knowledge of good and evil.

—GENESIS 2:7–9

YOU WOULD THINK THAT creating us is kind enough, but God, in his infinite grace, chose humanity out of all creation and placed them in his personally planted garden. We don't have much of a garden culture in North America, but most palaces and royal residences in Europe have some sort of private garden. This is where the king, queen, or whomever, can wander in the beauty of controlled and ordered nature. In Genesis, God is the gardener, and he plants a garden for humankind to enjoy. In this garden, God dwells with mankind and they enjoy relationship with him. He blesses them with the essentials of life, such as food, shelter, and water, because this was all they required. The rest of their desires were to be fulfilled by the bliss of relationship with a loving God who dwelt with them. There was no need for money, no need for the accumulation of possessions, no need for more stuff. They already possessed the earth and all that was in it as a gift of God.

However, they needed to remain faithful to God if they were to enjoy these blessings. In Genesis 2, God commands the first people to avoid eating from one tree or they "will certainly die" (Gen 2:17). In other words, if man is obedient to God's command, then this state of bliss in the garden will be his forever and ever. He will never taste death and will enjoy communion with God always. Yet, if he is disobedient to God's word then the gift of eternal life will be stripped from him and he will certainly die.

At this point we must understand that God is under no obligation to provide Adam and Eve with eternal life. It is his free decision to give man eternal life if they are obedient to his word. It's his free gift to them, his grace. Grace is an unavoidable fact throughout Scripture. We are consistently shown a God who bestows undeserved blessings on his people even though God is supremely powerful and under no obligation to do anything for anyone. He owes no one anything. All of his actions are a result of his gracious loving will and are completely unmerited. That is what grace means, unmerited favor. Therefore, when God removes these blessings from Adam and Eve for their disobedience he is not acting in an unjust or unfair way. The blessings are not owed to mankind in any way, but are a gift. We should reflect upon these gifts, being thankful that God is gracious.

Reflection Questions

1. What's so special about God putting people in a garden?
2. What do you think things would have been like had the first people remained in the garden?

Prayer

Lord, you gave people a garden and we long for that garden today. We eagerly await the day when you will return to dwell with your people for all eternity. Father, would you help us see your grace in every moment of our lives? Help us realize that you are the God of grace. Forgive us where we refuse to see your love and care. Amen.

Day 13

Q. Did Adam and Eve continue in the Garden?

A. No, Adam and Eve disobeyed God and were removed from the Garden.

Then the Lord God said to the woman, "What is this you have done?" The woman said, "The serpent deceived me, and I ate." So the Lord God said to the serpent, "Because you have done this, cursed are you above all livestock and all wild animals! You will crawl on your belly and you will eat dust all the days of your life. And I will put enmity between you and the woman, and between your offspring and hers; he will crush your head, and you will strike his heel."

—GENESIS 3:13–15

IN LOVE GOD CREATED a garden for Adam and Eve to enjoy for all eternity. This garden was a paradise full of delectable foods and untainted beauty, and there existed a harmony amongst the created order the likes of which we have not seen since. It was truly a paradise of God's gracious love for humanity to enjoy. Unfortunately, Adam and Eve did not remain faithful to God.

We see this in Genesis 3, where we are told that they were tempted by the serpent to disobey God's command regarding a certain fruit tree. Instead of listening to the God of love—who had given them paradise as their dwelling place—they decided that they knew better than God and ate of it. They bought into a lie, told to them by the prince of deception, that God was somehow withholding his full love and goodness from them by commanding them not to eat from this tree. Through this temptation of the evil one they fell into unbelief and questioned God's goodness towards them. As a result, they took, they ate, and their whole world fell apart.

Adam and Eve's resentment toward God by thinking that he was with-holding from them immediately backfired. Their innocence was lost, and they came to the sudden realization that they were naked and ashamed. They tried to hide themselves from God because of their newfound shame. The freedom they had to be seen by God was lost because of the stain of their sin. They lost paradise, breaking the bond between them and God. And because they rejected God through their disobedience, he cast them out of the garden. They lost the bliss of a perfect relationship with God, and they lost the physical sustenance the garden provided them. However, in the midst of the horrendous story of humanity's greatest calamity, God makes a promise. In Genesis 3:15, God curses the tempter and tells of a day when a man will crush his head as a symbol for the final defeat of the powers of evil. That man is Jesus Christ.

Reflection Questions

1. Have you ever thought of Adam and Eve's sin as unbelief?

2. How has Adam and Eve's sin shaped the world we live in?

Prayer

Heavenly Father, forgive our sins. We are just like Adam and Eve. We think that you are withholding your goodness from us all the time. We sin and disobey your commands. But, Father, we know that you have withheld nothing from us because you gave your Son for us. Thank you for sending Jesus to die for our sins. Let us trust in him more each day. Amen.

DAY 14

Q. What is sin?

A. Sin is any disloyalty to, or breaking of, God's commands.

The acts of the flesh are obvious: sexual immorality, impurity and debauchery; idolatry and witchcraft; hatred, discord, jealousy, fits of rage, selfish ambition, dissensions, factions and envy; drunkenness, orgies, and the like. I warn you, as I did before, that those who live like this will not inherit the kingdom of God.

—GALATIANS 5:19-21

OFTEN, WE THINK ABOUT sin as obvious evils or moral failures. We think about lying, cheating, stealing, killing, etc. And while there is no denying that these things are sins—and horrible ones at that—if we leave our definition of sin here it will be extremely deficient. These more heinous instances of sin blind us to so much of what sin actually is. Sin is not just breaking a list of rules we were told not to break. In fact, this characteristically unnuanced view is exactly what the evil one desires us to believe.

Instead, we need to define sin exclusively in terms of its relation to God. Otherwise, we run the risk of thinking sin is less than it actually is by removing its totalizing effects. We need to understand that sin is the breaking of God's commandments, which always begins with some sort of disloyalty to him. Sin is not only the act of adultery, or perjury, or murder, but is the hidden desire to break away from God's lordship that precedes those actions. Sin is both a particular outward action and an inward movement of the heart away from God. Anytime we treat our families, neighbors, or co-workers with less than the love of God, we are walking in sin. As we

27

commit those actions, we are disloyal to God in thought, word, and deed and thus we are doubly walking in sin. The outward action of evil deeds is nothing more than the revealing of the rejection of God's word in our hearts. Therefore, whenever we put anything in our life above or before our relationship with God, we are bound to commit evil deeds. All outward sins reveal our heart's true desires.

All of this sounds pretty stark. We can't even begin to fathom the depths of our own sinfulness, but the beautiful truth of the gospel is that God's love for us goes deeper than our sin. Jesus, God's son, was perfectly loyal to his heavenly Father, and thus, never committed any sins. He never lied, cheated, or stole. He never had an impure thought or motive. He never looked to anything other than God for satisfaction. And as a result, he loved everyone perfectly, without ever failing. He was the lamb without blemish whose perfection allowed him to be an atonement for our imperfection. Thus, on the cross, Christ took the penalty for sin that we deserved, enduring God's wrath towards sin. He defeated sin once and for all, and it is through him that sin has been defeated in our lives as well.

Reflection Questions

1. What do you tend to think of when you hear the word "sin?"
2. How are you loyal or disloyal to God?

Prayer

Lord Jesus, forgive us our sins we pray. You, Lord, are the God who graciously died for our sin, and we pray we might be reminded of that today. Amen.

Day 15

Q. What sin caused Adam and Eve to fall from the Garden?

A. The sin that caused Adam and Eve to fall from the Garden was eating the forbidden fruit.

Now the serpent was more crafty than any of the wild animals the Lord God had made. He said to the woman, "Did God really say, 'You must not eat from any tree in the garden'?" . . . When the woman saw that the fruit of the tree was good for food and pleasing to the eye, and also desirable for gaining wisdom, she took some and ate it. She also gave some to her husband, who was with her, and he ate it.

—GENESIS 3:1,6

WHY WAS EATING a piece of fruit such a big deal? It seems rather overkill that all of creation would be subjected to death and decay as a result of Adam and Eve's choice of dinner. Yet, when we examine this particular sin, it becomes clear that God's response was completely appropriate. We as modern readers have a lot of misunderstandings regarding this particular sin, all of which stem from our bad readings of the story. These readings make it seem like they misused some sort of magical fruit that God did not want them to have. However, the story itself is a rich source of theological truth and value.

In the story, God tells Adam and Eve what will happen to them if they eat the fruit: they will die. He is not trying to withhold something from them, but he's trying to protect them. His command to them is sort of like a parent who warns their child about running into a busy street. It's for their own good that they avoid this tree. So, when Adam and Eve do eat from the tree it's not as if the fruit magically did something to them that removed their eternal life. Rather, eating the forbidden fruit revealed something in their hearts about what they thought of God. Yes, Adam and Eve had been deceived by Satan, but their actions revealed more than an innocent error. Their actions revealed that they no longer trusted God to provide the best possible life for them. It revealed their disbelief in God's goodness and care. They spurned and stomped upon the love that he had shown them in the creation.

When we understand this we can see why God's response to their sin was not overkill. He was their Creator, he gave them every plant, every animal, and even a paradisal garden to dwell in. And despite all of this they were completely ungrateful and desired more. They decided that they knew better than God himself about what would make them happy. When Adam and Eve ate the forbidden fruit, it merely revealed the sin that they had already committed in their hearts. We could even go so far as to say that it revealed their hidden hatred of God's good protection and care over their lives.

Reflection Questions

1. Do you think eating the forbidden fruit was a big deal?
2. Have you ever thought about how their eating the fruit revealed the sin of their hearts?

Prayer

Father, we sin just like our first parents, Adam and Eve, sinned. Our hearts are not always set on loving you, thanking you, and worshiping you. Forgive us for these sins. Thank you that your Son Jesus has restored us to your kingdom. Would you reveal to us our heart's motive in what we do and turn it toward you alone? Amen.

DAY 16

Q. Did all people fall when Adam and Eve sinned?

A. Yes, when Adam and Eve sinned the punishment extended to everyone.

Therefore, just as sin entered the world through one man, and death through sin, and in this way death came to all people, because all sinned.

—ROMANS 5:12

ADAM AND EVE'S SIN was of such magnitude that its effects extended to all of humanity. When we look at Scripture it teaches us that sin permeated all of mankind after this one decisive event at the tree of knowledge. Immediately following the story of Adam and Eve's disobedience we find the story of history's first murder. Adam and Eve's child, Cain, harbors bitterness and resentment towards his brother, so much so that he kills him. The descent into total depravity and sinfulness is a quick one after the forbidden fruit is eaten. Thus, we cannot avoid the reality that sin and death extends to everyone as a result of Adam and Eve's sin. It is evident just by looking at the world.

In Christianity we call this concept *imputed guilt* and that simply means that in some way the punishment for Adam and Eve's sin is placed upon us as well. This might not seem fair to us, but it's actually perfectly just. It's not as if we are somehow free from sin. We all sin and commit horrible acts of disobedience against God's will. We do all sorts of terrible stuff as humanity. We bomb civilians, allow people to starve, turn a blind eye to the sanitation needs of those poorer than us, and so much more. Even in our daily lives we sin: we cheat, lie, steal, lust, are angered, and more. Clearly, we deserve the punishment for sin just as much as—if not more—than Adam and Eve.

Yet God is a God of grace and he made a way for the punishment of sin to be dealt with. God dealt with our sin through the cross of Jesus Christ. And when we put our hope in him the guilt that was imputed to us is taken away and we are forgiven all our sins. But God's saving work is more than simply forgiveness. He also gives us the righteousness of Christ. Christ, as the perfect man, gives us his perfect record so that when God looks at us he sees the spotless lamb, Jesus Christ. This is called *imputed righteousness* and what we learn from it is that God doesn't just forgives us, but he also gives us his own righteousness out of the abundance of his love. In Jesus we are made into new creations and freed from the law of sin and death forever.

Reflection Questions

1. What do *imputed guilt* and *imputed righteousness* mean?

2. Have you ever thought about how God doesn't just forgive your sins, but gives you Jesus Christ's perfect record?

Prayer

Heavenly Father, we justly deserve death for our sins. Yet, you forgive us in Jesus Christ. Thank you, Lord, that we are made perfect when we are found in Jesus Christ. We pray that you would help us to understand that we are new creations in him. Give us grace, we pray. Amen.

Day 17

Q. What happened to people after sin?

A. People are now marked by sin and death.

But the gift is not like the trespass. For if the many died by the trespass of the one man, how much more did God's grace and the gift that came by the grace of the one man, Jesus Christ, overflow to the many! Nor can the gift of God be compared with the result of one man's sin: The judgment followed one sin and brought condemnation, but the gift followed many trespasses and brought justification. For if, by the trespass of the one man, death reigned through that one man, how much more will those who receive God's abundant provision of grace and of the gift of righteousness reign in life through the one man, Jesus Christ!

—ROMANS 5:15–17

THE BIBLICAL PUNISHMENT FOR sin is clear: death. The result of Adam and Eve's sin in the garden was that the whole of the human race would suffer from an inherited sinfulness and thus would die. Therefore, we are all born destined for the grave. Despite this fact of human nature, there have always been people who argue that people are essentially good, that environment or other factors make them sin, that they are not sinners by nature. This is naïve and easily demonstrated to be wrong.

Every generation has an event in their memory which reveals the evil within the human heart. From 9/11 to the Holocaust, we all know of events which lift the veil from our eyes and show us the true nature of humanity. Even when we look at the world around us it is clear that sin has reached into everything people say and do. All we need to do is pick up any major newspaper and it becomes clear that sin and its consequences are everywhere. It's nearly impossible to deny the fact of humanity's universal sinfulness. Because of this, death reaches into every life. Death affects every human being equally, because we all sin equally. Sin and death truly are the great equalizers of humanity.

However, this is also what makes the biblical story so beautiful. The whole Bible is the story of God working in the world to finally bring an end to sin and death. The story begins with God promising Eve that a man would be born who would defeat the evil one. God then utilized Abraham, Moses, the people of Israel, David, and others to accomplish this promise. Finally, God sent his own Son, the Second Person of the Trinity, to rescue people from sin and death, once and for all. Jesus went to the cross, took the punishment for sin upon himself, died, and then rose again, defeating death. Now whoever believes that Jesus Christ is the Lord of the universe is free from the punishment of sin and will not experience the fullness of death. While Christians still die as a result of sin they do not die without hope. They die as men and women who will be raised up again to new life. They die as men and women who have defeated death in Jesus Christ.

Reflection Questions

1. Do you think people are basically good or basically sinful? Why?
2. What does God do to defeat sin and death?

Prayer

Gracious Father, we pray that you would forgive us. Every day we think and do things completely opposed to your ways. We don't love you or others how we should. Thank you, Lord, for you Son Jesus, who died for our sins so that we may be forgiven. We trust in him completely for forgiveness. Help us, Holy Spirit, to walk in new life. Amen.

DAY 18

Q. Why are people marked by sin and death?

A. People are marked by sin and death because they're born with original sin.

The fool says in his heart, "There is no God." They are corrupt, their deeds are vile; there is no one who does good. The Lord looks down from heaven on all mankind to see if there are any who understand, any who seek God. All have turned away, all have become corrupt; there is no one who does good, not even one.

—PSALM 14:1–3

THE THEOLOGICAL TERM WE use to explain why everything is so messed up in the world is *original sin*. As we have already seen, all people, without distinction, are marked by sin and death. We are all lost and subject to God's punishment for sin, apart from his saving work in us through his Son Jesus Christ, and by the indwelling power of the Holy Spirit. The idea of original sin explains why everyone is separated from God. It's because everyone without exception is born in sinfulness and has a natural propensity towards sin.

Theoretically this doctrine should be the most obvious to us in everyday life. Wherever we see evil in the world we should be able to point to original sin as the root cause. Every murder, every fraud, every genocide, every dictatorial government is evidence for original sin. However, despite its glaring obviousness, many fail to see humanity as being tainted with sin and having a capacity towards terrible evil. The idea that people are born fundamentally good and that teachers, parents, the environment we grow up in, and so on shape them towards evil is a very popular notion. We tend to see nurture as the reason for evil, not nature. The reason for this is because it's easier to believe that evil is a learned behavior than it is to look in the mirror and see oneself as holistically stained with vice. While this idea may be an easier pill to swallow, it's certainly not biblical, and neither does it adequately make sense of the world in which we live. We must be cautious not to disregard original sin because of our dislike for it. As Jeremiah poignantly warns, "The heart is deceitful above all things" (Jer 17:9).

Yet, rather than allow this truth of Scripture to condemn us we should see how it points to God's grace in Jesus Christ. We were born in sin, meaning we are completely unable to come to God. We were completely unable to do anything that might cause him to free us from our predicament. But God, being rich in mercy, accomplished the work for us so that we might be released from original sin and its penalties. This work was completed by Jesus Christ, who defeated all sin on the cross. God removed the stain of our original sin as a free gift towards us. Nothing we did could remove the stain of sinfulness, but God has. In this God shows his love for us. He not only removed the soiled garments we were trapped in but gave us completely new garments, free from all taint. Therefore, even though original sin can be a hard pill to swallow it ultimately points us to God's free gift of grace in Christ Jesus.

Reflection Questions

1. What is easier for you to grasp: original sin or that evil is a learned behavior?

2. How can we see God's grace in original sin?

Prayer

Father, before the foundation of the world you knew us and out of your grace rescued us through Jesus Christ. Forgive us, Lord, for our sins, and lead us not into temptation. We trust in the work of your Son Jesus, and believe he has rescued us from all sinfulness. Amen.

DAY 19

Q. What is bad about the fall?

**A. The fall means that people lost relationship with God, are
under his wrath, will experience death,
and the punishment of hell forever.**

*Then I saw a great white throne and him who was seated on it. The earth
and the heavens fled from his presence, and there was no place for them.
And I saw the dead, great and small, standing before the throne, and
books were opened. Another book was opened, which is the book of life.
The dead were judged according to what they had done as recorded in
the books . . . Anyone whose name was not found written in the book of
life was thrown into the lake of fire.*

—REVELATION 20:11‒12,15

WHY DOES THE PUNISHMENT for the fall seem so disproportionately harsh?
Why does the punishment last forever even though the sin Adam and Eve
committed only took a few seconds? These questions raise challenging and
perplexing realities which can only be understood when we examine who
it is that sin is committed against.

When the first people fell into sin their actions were committed against
God. The act of disobedience that they exhibited demonstrated that they
did not trust God's goodness or his word. Their sin was an act of cosmic
betrayal. They turned up the middle finger to their own Creator and demonstrated their treasonous attitude. Adam and Eve became the ungrateful
children who upon opening a gift toss it to the side as if it were a piece of

trash. They offended, were guilty against, and ungrateful to the good God who had given them everything.

Similarly, it's against this infinite and perfect God that we sin as well. All of our sin—every little bad thing we do—is an affront to the good God who created us and sustains us. Each act of disobedience we perform is a reenactment of the fall of Adam and Eve. Every time we are about to lie, cheat, steal, etc. we stand in the garden, so to speak, and are faced with the voice of the snake bidding us to take and eat. We are faced with a choice: to betray our Creator, or serve him and love him. It's his law we break when we sin and, therefore, we can rightly say that our sin is committed directly against God. It seems that we are not so different from our ancestors after all.

Yet, we still have not explored why the punishment for sin seems so harsh. Here we need to understand that God is infinite, in both time and space. He is beyond any sort of value we can attribute to him. He is infinitely valuable, holy, and righteous. Therefore, when we sin against an infinitely valuable, infinitely holy, and infinitely righteous God, the punishment must be infinite in scope. The punishment must fit the crime. When this is considered then it makes sense why the punishment of hell is forever. God is of such worth and value that the punishment for betrayal against him—the punishment for breaking his law—could not be otherwise.

Despite this fact it is important to remember that God does not desire that anyone should experience this punishment. He is not happy in his judgment against people. It's certain that some people will experience hell out of their own stubbornness to accept God's grace for them demonstrated on the cross. These people remain locked in their own sinfulness by their own choice, forever rejecting God. However, it is not God's desire that they do this. His desire is to see all people come to accept the forgiveness of sins made possible in Jesus Christ (2 Pet 3:9). This is God's ultimate hope for a broken world.

Reflection Questions

1. What do you find most difficult about the biblical teaching on hell?

2. Do you see God as a God of grace who desires that no one suffer eternal damnation?

Prayer

Lord, we pray that you would help us understand the difficult doctrine of hell. Be gracious and merciful towards us as we wrestle with this teaching. Help us to humbly submit to your word and accept all that we find there. Remind us of the grace shown to us in Jesus Christ. Amen.

DAY 20

Q. Did God leave people to die in sin?

A. No, God elected some people through Jesus to deliver them from sin and bring them into salvation.

For he chose us in him before the creation of the world to be holy and blameless in his sight. In love he predestined us for adoption to sonship through Jesus Christ, in accordance with his pleasure and will—to the praise of his glorious grace, which he has freely given us in the One he loves.

—EPHESIANS 1:4-6

EVERYONE, WITHOUT DISTINCTION, IS subject to the punishment for sin. Not only does the Bible teach that we are sinful from birth, but it also teaches us that we all commit sinful actions: "for all have sinned and fall short of the glory of God" (Rom 3:23). Not one person, on the whole face of the earth, is without sin and deserving of God's saving work. When we look at the world, we see inequality in wealth, inequality in opportunities, and inequality based on race, gender, or class, but inequality does not exist in the realm of sin and death. In this realm we find ourselves all equally deserving of God's wrath.

This is precisely why it is so astounding that God made the conscious choice to save some people from this perilous future. In his eternal decree—his divine free choice—he chose to bring the gift of salvation to some of these wretched people. This idea is best expressed using the word *election* which describes how God chooses some of us to partake in his saving work. And if God's saving work is extended to the people that he chooses then it is fair to say that this work is a free gift of grace. A free gift, not given to us because of our great performance, or because of something within us, but because of God's gracious love towards us, which is fully displayed in the person and work of Jesus Christ. God's plan to save those whom he desired was accomplished through the death of his Son and his being raised to new life.

The fact that God has saved us as an act of free grace has many implications and it should bring us great joy. First, we can know that we have been chosen and adopted by the God of the whole universe. We are now his sons and daughters in Christ and this should give us a great confidence, because now that we know God is for us, well then, "who can be against us?" (Rom 8:31). Secondly, we can take joy in knowing that we don't need to earn God's favor, but can rest assured in the reality that God's favor has been lavishly poured upon us already as we trust in his Son. Our work is not meant to be a burdensome toiling to gain the divine smile towards us, but our work is a faithful obedience because of the divine smile upon us.

Reflection Questions

1. Have you ever thought about how everyone equally deserves the punishment for sin?

2. How does it make you feel to know that God chose to save you?

Prayer

Lord Almighty, you are the God who before the foundations of the world decided to rescue me from my sins. There is nothing I have done to deserve this. I can offer you nothing to earn this. You saved me through your choice and showed your love for me in Jesus. Thank you for this love. Amen.

DAY 21

Q. Who is the savior of God's elect?

A. The savior is the Lord Jesus Christ, the eternal Son of God, who became man and died for our sins.

For God so loved the world that he gave his one and only Son, that whoever believes in him shall not perish but have eternal life. For God did not send his Son into the world to condemn the world, but to save the world through him. Whoever believes in him is not condemned, but whoever does not believe stands condemned already because they have not believed in the name of God's one and only Son.

—JOHN 3:16–18

NOW THAT WE KNOW that God, in eternity past, chose some people to be saved from their sins, it is fair to ask: How is this accomplished? It most certainly is not accomplished through our works. Nothing we do can atone for our sin before God. As discussed previously, God's infinite holiness means our sin deserves infinite wrath. Thus, trying to *earn* salvation is like trying to pay off the United States deficit working at McDonald's part-time. It's an impossible task. The only real possibility for salvation then (apart from God) is to live a perfectly sinless life from the moment of birth till the day of death. However, original sin makes this an impossibility. We are irrevocably marked with the scourge of sin, and our hearts lead us into all sorts of sin. So, if it's impossible to be saved through our work, then how are we saved? What did God decree within the relationship of the Trinity as the way of salvation for his elect?

He decreed that his eternal Son, revealed in the man Jesus Christ, would die for the sins of the world. It was God's will that he would send his Son into the world for the salvation of sin. Every member of the Godhead was a willing participant in this plan. It was the Son's will that he would submit to this plan of redemption and it was the Holy Spirit's will to make this salvation known to those that were chosen as God's elect. Yet, how does this work? How is the sacrifice of God's Son enough to atone for the sins of the elect? Simply put, Jesus Christ was both fully man and fully God. As man he was able to walk the perfectly sinless life no one ever could, and as God his righteousness was infinite in scope, so much so that the infinite debt of humanity was fulfilled by him.

It is because of this that there is no way to heaven apart from Jesus Christ. He is the appointed means for the world's salvation. Only he could fulfill the righteous requirements of God's law as God himself. Only he could offer himself up as the perfect sacrifice because his righteousness exceeded the value of the debt we owed in our sin. Jesus Christ is the appointed means to salvation and it is Jesus Christ alone who we must look to for salvation. In fact, to look for salvation in anything else is a rejection of God's plan for the universe. It's a rejection of God's own Son. All those who look to Christ alone will not be denied the salvation he offers. He is the only road leading to heaven and thus, to depart along any other path is a grave error ending in eternal damnation.

Reflection Questions

1. How does Jesus meet the requirements for our salvation?
2. What does it mean that Jesus is the only way to salvation?

Prayer

Heavenly Father, we pray that you would help us to understand these things. We know we can't fully grasp the mysteries of your existence, but we pray that you would help us see the truths of your workings revealed to us in Scripture. Let us trust in your Son. Lord, give us eyes to see and ears to hear your truth. Amen.

Day 22

Q. How did Jesus Christ, the Son of God, become man?

A. Jesus Christ, the Son of God, was born to the virgin Mary
by the Holy Spirit and took on human flesh,
yet he was without sin.

*So Joseph also went up from the town of Nazareth in Galilee to Judea,
to Bethlehem the town of David, because he belonged to the house and
line of David. He went there to register with Mary, who was pledged to
be married to him and was expecting a child. While they were there, the
time came for the baby to be born, and she gave birth to her firstborn,
a son. She wrapped him in cloths and placed him in a manger, because
there was no guest room available for them.*

—LUKE 2:4-7

WE ALL KNOW AND love the Christmas story. Jesus Christ, the eternal Son
of God, became a man in the most profound way possible, as an infant.
We've seen TV specials and Christmas plays which show the birth of Christ
in dramatic fashion. And it is common that these renditions on TV or the
stage reflect the lowly status of his birth. They highlight the fact that he was
born in a manger, or that there was not enough space at the inn, so that we
might witness the meekness of Christ and sympathize with the characters
of the story who struggle to find comfort during the delivery of this child.
While this is a necessary part of the Christmas story—which can teach us
a lot about the nature of God and his workings in the world—at the same

time, we need to be cautious that we do not miss the opportunity to reflect on the greatness of God present in this birth.

When we say that the Son of God became man it needs to be understood that this is the same Son present before the foundation of the world with the Father. The same Son who participated in the preparation of the plan of salvation in eternity past. The same Son who was active in creating the universe by his word of power. The same Son who is "the radiance of God's glory and the exact representation of his being, sustaining all things by his powerful word" (Heb 1:3).

This same Son is born a man, fully human and fully divine. This is an astounding reality. No amount of words will ever do it justice. God became man in Jesus Christ. No TV rendition or stage play showing the birth of Christ will ever capture the gravity of this event. The Infinite One took on our finitude in his human nature so that our infinite debt might be dealt with decisively in his life, death, and resurrection. On a quiet night of his own creation, under the starry host that he set in place, to a mother he knit together in the womb, Jesus Christ, the God man, was born.

Reflection Questions

1. What is your favorite part of the Christmas story?
2. What does it mean that God became man?

Prayer

Lord, we worship you and praise you for the amazing reality that in Jesus Christ we see God become man. Father, thank you for sending your Son in this way. Thank you for allowing us to see your grace in him. Forgive us where we ignore the wonder of this miracle. Amen.

DAY 23

Q. What offices does Christ fulfill as our savior?

A. Christ fulfills the offices of a prophet, a priest, and a king.

For I gave them the words you gave me and they accepted them. They knew with certainty that I came from you, and they believed that you sent me. I pray for them. I am not praying for the world, but for those you have given me, for they are yours. All I have is yours, and all you have is mine. And glory has come to me through them.

—JOHN 17:8–10

WHETHER WE REALIZE IT or not, everyone needs a prophet, a priest, and a king. A prophet's main role is to communicate the words of God to his people. He brings God's word, under God's guidance, to the people so that they might know him. If we were left without prophets, we would be without God's word. Hence, most religions have some sort of prophet figure as the messenger of God for them.

A priest's role is to be a mediator between God and man. He intercedes with the deity on behalf of the people so that they might secure that particular god's favor. In the Old Testament Scriptures, priests offered sacrifices for the sins of the people at the temple. Thus, since we all sin, we all need someone to continuously make offerings on our behalf.

A king governs and rules his people. The function of a king in the Old Testament was to rule under God's word. Good kings would do this with perfect justice, executing God's will for the sake of the people. Even today we long for a good king to rule over us. How else would you characterize our hope in political leaders? We desire a king, a ruler of justice, who will make the world right.

We long for these roles to be fulfilled, but often the people who take them up fall short. A just ruler may come around, but they do not, and cannot, execute perfect justice. A prophet might rise up amongst us, claiming to bring God's word to us, but yet ends up having everyone drink the Kool-Aid, so to speak. Priests may abound, but the moral failures associated with them is an insurmountable obstacle in taking them seriously.

Yet when we look to Jesus Christ, the Son of God become man, we see these roles completely fulfilled. He is the perfect prophet who makes God known to us and speaks the words of God himself. He is the perfect priest who gave not only a sacrifice, but gave his very body up as an offering for our sin. He is the perfect king who was raised from the dead and ascended into heaven to rule over the whole universe at the right hand of the Father. All of these roles are forever fulfilled in him. Every longing we have for spirituality, justice, and satisfaction of guilt is completed in him. Jesus—as prophet, priest, and king—completely satisfies our deepest human longings for a just, peaceful, and blissful world.

Reflection Questions

1. What role—prophet, priest, or king—stands out to you most? Why?

2. How does Jesus fulfill the role that stands out to you?

Prayer

O Father, thank you for your Son Jesus, who is the perfect prophet, priest, and king. Speak to us, Lord, through him, forgive us in him, and lead us by him. Amen.

Day 24

Q. How does Christ fulfill the role of a prophet?

A. Christ fulfills the role of a prophet by revealing God's will through his word and by his Spirit.

In the past God spoke to our ancestors through the prophets at many times and in various ways, but in these last days he has spoken to us by his Son, whom he appointed heir of all things, and through whom also he made the universe. The Son is the radiance of God's glory and the exact representation of his being, sustaining all things by his powerful word. After he had provided purification for sins, he sat down at the right hand of the Majesty in heaven.

—HEBREWS 1:1–3

WHEN WE LOOK AT Scripture, we find God speaking to his people through the prophets. These prophets heard God's word and relayed it to the people of Israel so that they too would know God's word. Moses brought the people of Israel the law as he heard it from God on Sinai, Jonah brought God's word to Nineveh so that they would repent from their sin, and Elijah spoke to the evil King Ahab at God's prompting.

Likewise, as we turn to the New Testament, we see God speak to his people through this means as well, but this time through his own Son. Christ is the perfect prophet who communicates God's words to us so that we might know him and draw close to him. Jesus is not like the other prophets who merely heard God's word; Christ was with God from eternity past and is himself God. John 1:18 says, "No one has ever seen God, but the one and only Son, who is himself God and is in closest relationship with the Father, has made him known." It is Jesus that makes God known to us and thus he speaks to us as the perfect prophet.

Yet, most of us have never seen Jesus face to face. Most of us haven't spoken to him as we speak with a friend who is physically present with us. So how does he speak to us as a prophet today? He reveals to us his word, the Bible, so that we may see him amongst its pages. His Holy Spirit works in our hearts so that we might have ears to hear and eyes to see what God's word says to us and to show us Christ throughout the whole of Scripture. Which is why the Bible is such an important aspect of our walk as Christians. In Scripture, we believe that Jesus is speaking to us as a prophet revealing God's word through the indwelling Holy Spirit. Therefore, we should not neglect this great book that has been given to us. It is powerful and effective to change lives as the Spirit works through it.

Reflection Questions

1. How is Jesus a prophet?
2. Why is Scripture so important for our walk with Jesus today?

Prayer

Father, your words are more precious to us than anything else we could imagine. Forgive us for the times we neglect the Bible and refuse to recognize Jesus in it. We pray that the Holy Spirit would help us see how Jesus speaks on all its pages. Amen.

Day 25

Q. How does Christ fulfill the role of a priest?

A. Christ fulfills the role of a priest by offering himself up as a sacrifice for our sins and in making continual prayers for us.

Therefore, since we have a great high priest who has ascended into heaven, Jesus the Son of God, let us hold firmly to the faith we profess. For we do not have a high priest who is unable to empathize with our weaknesses, but we have one who has been tempted in every way, just as we are—yet he did not sin. Let us then approach God's throne of grace with confidence, so that we may receive mercy and find grace to help us in our time of need.

—HEBREWS 4:14-16

TODAY THE IDEA OF a priest evokes images in our minds of men in long black robes with strange white collars around their necks. It tends to spark images in our minds of the confessional or a grand Catholic cathedral. Perhaps, because of the grave errors of a few, it even sparks images in our minds of abuse and disgust. These images from movies and pop culture mean that, for many of us, priests are simply caricatures in our minds rather than real live human beings we see on a day-to-day basis. However, we need to be careful that we do not let these images of the priesthood color our view of Jesus Christ, especially when we refer to him as fulfilling the role of a priest.

Some historical context may help us to see better what Scripture means when it refers to Jesus as the great high priest. In the ancient world, a priest's job was to act as a middleman between the people and their god. A good example of this principle can be seen in the Bible regarding ancient Israel. There the priest would perform ritual sacrifices to atone for the sins of the people and for themselves. The priest's role was to point the people to God's forgiveness for them through these sacrifices. Essentially the priest performed a ritual meant to show the people—specifically the Israelites—that their sin was forgiven through the death of another, in this case the sacrificial animal.

Therefore, when we say that Jesus fulfills the role of priest, we're saying that Jesus acts as someone who offers up sacrifices on our behalf. Somebody who points to God's forgiving love through sacrifice. Yet, unlike the Old Testament priests Jesus didn't offer up a lamb as a sacrifice, but he offered up himself as the perfect sacrifice for sin. And through this perfect sacrifice Jesus bought forgiveness for us. So, when we look at the sacrificial system in the Old Testament now, we are seeing a foreshadowing of the great sacrifice of Jesus Christ for our sins. As we read about the Levitical priest sacrificing the lamb upon the altar, we see a picture of Christ's work on our behalf. We can see, with the knowledge we now have, that Christ is the ultimate sacrificial lamb who takes away the sins of the world.

Thus, all of the promises of forgiveness in the Bible find their yes and amen in Christ. Not only that, but Jesus, the perfect priest, continues his priestly work by interceding for us in prayer as it says in Scripture, "and is also interceding for us" (Rom 8:34). Jesus, as the perfect priest, offered himself as the perfect sacrifice and continues his priestly ministry by interceding for us to the Father.

Reflection Questions

1. What do you think of when you hear the word "priest?"

2. What does it mean for you practically that Jesus is the perfect priest?

Prayer

Father in Heaven, we pray that we might see Jesus as our true priest. Don't allow us to look at other things to somehow draw us closer to you. Let us fix our eyes on Jesus alone as the perfecter of our faith. Lord, we pray that we might understand the depth of your love for us through the sacrifice Jesus made on our behalf. Amen.

DAY 26

Q. How does Christ fulfill the role of a king?

A. Christ fulfills the role of a king by ruling, defending us, and defeating all his enemies.

He raised Christ from the dead and seated him at his right hand in the heavenly realms, far above all rule and authority, power and dominion, and every name that is invoked, not only in the present age but also in the one to come. And God placed all things under his feet and appointed him to be head over everything for the church.

—EPHESIANS 1:20B-22

THE IDEA OF A king seems barbaric to most of us in the modern world. Today when we think of kings we think of despots, dictators, and tyrants. We think of the evil king we see on the silver screen, who rules with injustice and cares little for his people, if at all. We may even think of examples from history such as Henry VIII, Pharaoh, or Herod to bolster our view that kings are bad, neglecting to think of good kings, such as Charlemagne. This cultural trend within the democratic West means that we view kingship as dangerously close to tyranny. We tend to go by the axiom "absolute power corrupts absolutely," but does it necessarily? Does not mitigated power equally corrupt?

It should seem obvious to most of us by now in the democratic West that something is wrong. The ideals of democracy which have been built up in our heads are beginning to decay. With elections being swayed by other nations for the purpose of destabilization, with bureaucratic procedures sucking the life out of rather simple tasks, and with leaders who seem more buffoonish than some kings throughout history, our trust in democracy is beginning to wane. Simply put, as we weigh the democratic system in the scales of goodness and justice, we find it leaning ever more away from these values. Our ideal of democracy is being challenged and likewise our idolatrous relationship with it is equally challenged.

Yet, if there were a good king, if there were a ruler who held absolute power but never used it for personal gain, acted with justice, protected his people from their enemies, and was successful in all his good endeavors then wouldn't the idea of kingship be redeemed? If this were possible then would it not challenge our idolatrous relationship with democracy? Would it not challenge our fears of an authoritarian ruler knowing this king would be good? Our answer to these questions is "yes and amen." And these positive answers are possible because in Jesus Christ this is the kind of king we have.

After Jesus' death and resurrection, he ascended to the right hand of the Father, where he now rules the universe in his love and grace. He is perfectly just, he defends us, watching over us constantly, and he has defeated our enemy—the evil one—by his death. And while the kingdom of God has not yet been fully realized here on earth, we can know that Jesus Christ will bring about a final victory over sin and death. When that happens, God will dwell with us and Christ will be the perfect king, ruling over all his people for all eternity in absolute perfection. As Christians we long for this. In a world where political opinion is used as a weapon to divide people and drive them into violence, war, and hatred for their brothers, we long for peace and justice to be upheld. We long for a world that is a united utopia of mankind coexisting in eternal joy. And if this is what we want then we must realize that only Jesus can usher this world in. Therefore, let us worship him as the mighty king of creation.

Reflection Questions

1. Does a good king sound like an oxymoron to you?
2. If Jesus is our good king, then how does this challenge our idolatrous relationship with democracy?

Prayer

Lord, you are the King over all creation. We worship you and honor you as the only one who brings lasting peace to a divided world. Father, help us see the kingship of Jesus and trust in his sovereign rule today. Do not let us trust in any power but in Christ alone. Amen.

DAY 27

Q. What is Jesus Christ's humiliation?

A. Jesus Christ's humiliation is his leaving heaven, becoming a man, and dying on the cross.

Who, being in very nature God, did not consider equality with God something to be used to his own advantage; rather, he made himself nothing by taking the very nature of a servant, being made in human likeness. And being found in appearance as a man, he humbled himself by becoming obedient to death—even death on a cross!

—PHILIPPIANS 2:6–8

AS WE READ THE Gospels it is important for us to hold a tension within our minds: the tension between Jesus Christ's divinity and his humanity. As we turn to the Gospels, we see the God-man—the one who was present with God and was God before the foundation of the world—coming into the world as a helpless infant. We are brought face to face with the divine who now has to grow up and experience all the awkward developmental stages of life. We see the mighty king of the universe who upholds everything by his word of power, dying on a cross. The Creator of all things hanged on a tree of his own creation. In his sovereign will he sustained the life of the cattle whose skin would be used as the leather in the whip that tore his own skin. In these historical moments we are forced to ponder the humiliation of Jesus Christ.

The Son of God, very God of very God, left heaven in all his glory and became a man. He "had no beauty or majesty to attract us to him" and "nothing in his appearance that we should desire him" (Isa 53:2). He humbled himself in both his stature and through the life he lived on earth. He allowed himself to experience temptation and pain throughout his life. He allowed wicked men to falsely accuse him, even though he did nothing wrong, so that he might be condemned to death. He allowed himself to be sentenced to death by crucifixion and he gave up his life nailed to a piece of wood. As passersby looked upon his lifeless body, they unwittingly witnessed the God of the whole universe hanging by his hands and feet on a tree.

Yet in this humiliation God worked out his plan of salvation for his people. It was in Jesus Christ's humiliation that the plan of salvation was fulfilled: "God made him who had no sin to be sin for us, so that in him we might become the righteousness of God" (2 Cor 5:21). Therefore, let us soberly remember the weight of Christ's humiliation and rejoice in the upside-down nature of God's plan to save his people.

Reflection Questions

1. What stands out to you about Jesus Christ's humiliation?

2. What does it say about Jesus that he was willing to suffer this humiliation?

Prayer

Heavenly Father, thank you for your Son Jesus Christ, who humbled himself for our sake. We are completely unworthy of the love that Jesus showed us by coming and dying for us. Help us, Lord, to humble ourselves before you just as Jesus Christ humbled himself in his life. Amen.

Day 28

Q. What is Jesus Christ's exaltation?

A. Jesus Christ's exaltation is his rising from the dead, ascending to heaven, and ruling over everything.

Therefore God exalted him to the highest place and gave him the name that is above every name, that at the name of Jesus every knee should bow, in heaven and on earth and under the earth, and every tongue acknowledge that Jesus Christ is Lord, to the glory of God the Father.

—PHILIPPIANS 2:9–11

JESUS CHRIST, IN HIS humiliation, was made low, even to the point of death. Yet, in his exaltation Christ was lifted up beyond everything else. As the God of the universe, death could not overcome him. From the grave he was raised to new life "because it was impossible for death to keep its hold on him" (Acts 2:24). Through this he became the first fruits of the resurrection that he promised to his followers. After forty days of teaching his disciples, Jesus Christ ascended to the right hand of the Father. Here, in his completely glorified state, he rules at God's right hand, sovereignly overseeing the whole of the universe as our great King.

In Jesus Christ's exaltation we see his defeat of sin and death, his complete sovereign rule, and his love for us in that rule. It's at God's right hand that Jesus Christ intercedes for us, working out all things for our good (Rom 8:28). He brings our prayers to God, and acts in his exalted state as our Great High Priest. Likewise, he acts as a prophet in sending the Holy Spirit to dwell within us and open the Scriptures to us so that we might know God's word. All of these things are made possible because of Jesus Christ's exaltation to the right hand of the Father.

This is why it is so important for us to remember that we don't worship a God who simply died for us. Jesus is not only alive in our hearts but is really and fully alive at the right hand of God. We shouldn't think that Christ merely embodied a principle of love through his death. We shouldn't think that his resurrection and ascension are miracles too great for history to acknowledge. We cannot accept this. Without his exaltation we worship a mere fantasy of the imagination and we are utterly without hope for a future life. Christ's exaltation is living proof of the defeat of death in our own lives. It is by his exaltation that we have assurance of the resurrection. Through it we know that we will be raised to new life with him when he returns on that final day. Let us not cast aside this foundational doctrine; instead let us turn to Scripture where we see it evidently displayed.

Reflection Questions

1. Had you ever heard of Christ's exaltation before? What does it include?

2. Why is Christ's exaltation so important for Christians to believe?

Prayer

Exalted Lord, we worship you and praise you for your good works in our lives. You sovereignly rule all things for our good. Help us Lord, by your Spirit, to see your greatness in Jesus Christ. Amen.

DAY 29

Q. How do we have our sins forgiven?

A. We have our sins forgiven by believing in Jesus' work through the Holy Spirit.

If you declare with your mouth, "Jesus is Lord," and believe in your heart that God raised him from the dead, you will be saved. For it is with your heart that you believe and are justified, and it is with your mouth that you profess your faith and are saved.

—ROMANS 10:9–10

IT IS ONLY THROUGH Jesus Christ that are our sins forgiven. It is only by his work on the cross and through his resurrection that we are saved. Yet, how is this forgiveness applied to our lives? This is a fair question to ask and the answer is twofold. First, salvation comes through the work of God in our hearts by bringing us to belief in Jesus through the Holy Spirit. We don't work our way up to belief in Jesus Christ, but it begins and ends as a work of God in our life. He softens our hearts and shows us Jesus Christ through his Holy Spirit. Secondly, forgiveness takes place when we confess our belief in Jesus as Lord and Savior. Again, a true confession of faith is only possible through the work of the Holy Spirit bringing us to belief in Jesus. Therefore, forgiveness of sins comes by believing in Jesus Christ through the work of the Holy Spirit.

However, this creates a problem. How can we know who the Holy Spirit has wrought this work in? And the answer is that we can't. We are not in a place to judge the secrets of the human heart, only God can do that. When we look at others, we simply cannot know whether the Holy

Spirit has worked in this way or not. Therefore, we must rely on a person's confession of faith in Jesus Christ. Romans 10:9 says, "If you declare with your mouth, 'Jesus is Lord,' and believe in your heart that God raised him from the dead, you will be saved." Since we can hear a confession of faith, but cannot see a person's heart, we rely upon the confession.

Salvation is certainly an overt work of God in the life of the elect. We are saved the moment God works in our hearts and brings us to a place of confession. And this means that we can be completely certain of our salvation in Jesus when we put our trust in him for, "Everyone who calls on the name of the Lord will be saved" (Rom 10:13). We don't need to doubt whether or not we are saved after we believe in our hearts and confess with our mouth. Falling into sin will happen, but this does not discount the previous work of God. If this were true, then certainly we would all be lost, but thanks be to God that when we believe in our hearts and confess with our mouths the promise of forgiveness is given to us forever and always.

Reflection Questions

1. How can you remind yourself that you have been forgiven by Jesus Christ even when you don't feel it?

2. What are some Scripture passages you could memorize to remind yourself of the promises of Jesus Christ for you?

Prayer

Gracious Lord, you alone are the God who saves. You work salvation in our hearts through the Holy Spirit. Thank you for your Son Jesus, who died for our sins. We confess that he is the Lord of our lives. Help us where we doubt our salvation. Fill us with your Spirit and remind us of your great love for us. Amen.

DAY 30

Q. How does the Holy Spirit work in us to show us Jesus?

A. The Holy Spirit works in us to bring about faith in Jesus and unites us to him.

I will sprinkle clean water on you, and you will be clean; I will cleanse you from all your impurities and from all your idols. I will give you a new heart and put a new spirit in you; I will remove from you your heart of stone and give you a heart of flesh. And I will put my Spirit in you and move you to follow my decrees and be careful to keep my laws.

—EZEKIEL 36:25-27

ONE OF THE TROPES that undergirds the home renovation show is the *fixer-upper*, where a prospective owner buys a house that needs a lot of work before it can be made into a real, livable home. It may need to have its walls torn down, new paint, new flooring, a kitchen renovation, or other repairs before its potential is fully realized. So, the property owner begins to renovate, transforming the house from something shabby and dreary into a work of art filled with beauty. He transforms it into a home.

This is a good analogy for how God works in us through the Holy Spirit. Every single one of us is a fixer-upper. We have been so marred by sin—we are such broken creatures—that God must enter into our hearts and begin the renovation process. He may need to tear down the idols in our life in order to teach us to worship him alone. He might need to rip off the things we were clinging to for our rest and security. He may need to chisel away at our hearts and remove the calloused pieces which prevented us from loving as he loves. But as the Holy Spirit accomplishes his work in our hearts, he brings about faith in Jesus, making this fixer-upper his home. This is one of the great truths of Christianity, that the Holy Spirit dwells within us as we believe in Jesus and unites us forever to him. God dwells in his people.

Yet, the work of the Holy Spirit is not complete after we come to believe in Jesus Christ. Even after he has moved into the house, he continues to fix it up, changing and building as need be to bring us into deeper relationship with God. Therefore, we should find encouragement in the knowledge that God himself dwells in us, transforming our hearts by his Spirit, and unites us to Jesus Christ, who is seated at God's right hand.

Reflection Questions

1. Do you see yourself as a fixer-upper? Why or why not?
2. What does it mean to have the Holy Spirit dwell within you and to be united to Christ?

Prayer

Father, we are all sinners. Every single one of us is a fixer-upper. We don't deserve the love you have shown us through Jesus Christ. Lord, forgive us when we take this grace for granted. Help us to see the love of Jesus anew today. Amen.

DAY 31

Q. What is effectual calling?

A. Effectual calling is the Holy Spirit convicting us of sin, transforming our minds to see what Jesus has done for us, and allowing us to accept Jesus' forgiveness.

Then he said to me, "Prophesy to these bones and say to them, 'Dry bones, hear the word of the Lord! This is what the Sovereign Lord says to these bones: "I will make breath enter you, and you will come to life. I will attach tendons to you and make flesh come upon you and cover you with skin; I will put breath in you, and you will come to life. Then you will know that I am the Lord."'

—EZEKIEL 37:4–6

GENERALLY SPEAKING, DEAD THINGS are an unresponsive lot. If you see something dead and attempt to get its attention, nothing will happen. With its eyes glazed over, a frigid cold body, and completely devoid of all life, the dead just lie there. Unfortunately for us, this is the imagery the Bible uses to describe our spiritual condition while we are walking in sin. The apostle Paul compares us to the dead before the Holy Spirit awoke us to the power of God. We see this when he writes, "As for you, you were dead in your transgressions and sin" (Eph 2:1). Our own sin has rendered us dead to the things of God. And in our deathly stupor—that is analogous to death itself—we're unresponsive and incapable of being brought back to life of our own volition.

With this being our condition before God it would seem as if there is little hope of salvation at all for us. Dead things cannot do anything, and because we are dead we likewise cannot do anything to change this condition. Behold, we are screwed! The only solution to this conundrum is a mighty work of God that brings us life so that we might receive his forgiveness in Jesus. Therefore, the Holy Spirit needs to work in our hearts so that we can be brought to life. This means that the change that takes place within us when we believe in Jesus is not simply a small change in direction but is a drastic change from death to life. In theology we call this effectual calling.

Effectual calling is the work the Holy Spirit performs in our hearts to bring us to life. He works in us to convict us of our sinfulness, he transforms our minds so that we can see what Jesus has done for us on the cross, and he allows us to accept the forgiveness Jesus offers. And once the work of effectual calling has been completed, and we come to confess Jesus as Lord, we are made "alive with Christ" (Eph 2:5). All of this reminds us that God's salvation for us is an act of grace. It is through the work of Jesus and by the Holy Spirit's work in our hearts that we are saved.

Reflection Questions

1. How does the Bible describe us before we believe in Jesus?
2. What changes does the Holy Spirit work in our hearts?

Prayer

Father, you raise the dead. And just as you raised your Son Jesus to new life, you raise us to new life. Lord, we praise you for bringing new life into our hearts. We praise you for the future new life you will bring to our bodies. You are the Almighty who resurrects the dead. Remind us of your grace towards us today. Amen.

Day 32

Q. What benefits come with following Jesus?

A. Those who follow Jesus benefit by being justified before God, being adopted into his holy family, and by being sanctified throughout life.

But when the set time had fully come, God sent his Son, born of a woman, born under the law, to redeem those under the law, that we might receive adoption to sonship. Because you are his sons, God sent the Spirit of his Son into our hearts, the Spirit who calls out, "Abba, Father."

—GALATIANS 4:4–6

SOMETIMES WE'RE AFRAID TO talk about the benefits that come with following Jesus because we are worried that we will overpromise on what it means to follow Jesus. We can be overly fearful, for instance, that ruminating on the benefits that come with following Jesus will lead people to believe that all their diseases will be healed, they will be made rich, and all their dreams will come true. The reason for this fear is valid. We do not want a misunderstanding of gospel benefits to lead people into believing a false gospel—in particular the prosperity gospel. We are rightfully fearful that misapplied teaching on the benefits of following Jesus will lead people into a false belief that wealth, success, and health are the outcomes of their faith. We are fearful that people will be ill-equipped to deal with their daily crosses because they interpret the benefits of following Jesus in material terms alone.

Yet, this fear of misapplication should not prevent us from discussing the benefits we see in Scripture that come with following Jesus. Following

Jesus Christ in this life does come with rewards. In fact, I would argue that it is impossible for the Christian to overpromise when it comes to the benefits that Jesus bestows upon us through belief in him. If for no other reason, it is simply because we cannot even begin to fathom the wonderful reality of the heavenly rewards that await us. These benefits will be so amazing that any earthly treasure will be a mere shadow in comparison to them. So let us not be fearful to discuss the benefits that come with following Jesus.

Primarily, the benefits of following Jesus come in the form of justification, adoption, and sanctification. Each of these will be discussed in the following questions-and-answers, but for now it is sufficient to know that there really are benefits to following Jesus Christ as Lord and Savior. We, as present believers in Jesus Christ, can know that no matter what, these three things are true of us. It doesn't matter whether we are in the midst of suffering or experiencing joy unimaginable, it is always true that we are forgiven and made righteous before God, that we are his adopted sons and daughters whom he loves, and that we are set apart as holy. It is God's will that these benefits are bestowed upon everyone who trusts in Jesus Christ. Therefore, rest assured that these benefits are true of anyone who believes, even you.

Reflection Questions

1. Have you ever thought about the benefits that belief in Jesus brings?

2. What benefit stands out most to you and brings you the most encouragement?

Prayer

Heavenly Father, you have chosen in your goodness to bestow all these benefits upon us when we believe in Jesus Christ. Thank you for your forgiveness and righteousness. Thank you for making us your sons and daughters. Thank you for setting us apart as your holy people. Remind us constantly of these benefits and allow us to rest in the knowledge of them. Amen.

DAY 33

Q. What is justification?

A. Justification is when we are forgiven our sins and receive Christ's perfection as our own.

This righteousness is given through faith in Jesus Christ to all who be-lieve. There is no difference between Jew and Gentile, for all have sinned and fall short of the glory of God, and all are justified freely by his grace through the redemption that came by Christ Jesus.

—ROMANS 3:22-24

THE MORE WE CONTEMPLATE the benefits that belief in Jesus brings, while at the same time contemplating the immense cost Jesus paid to secure these benefits, the more we understand his love for us. Jesus was not like one of us, tainted by sin and walking in it moment by moment. Rather, Jesus was completely free from sin. There was never a moment in Jesus' life when he gave in to temptation, never a moment where he walked away from God's perfect law. And Jesus, in his perfection, was killed by us: ruthless, idolatrous murderers. He was hung up on a tree and became a curse for our sakes: "Anyone who is hung on a pole is under God's curse" (Deut 21:23).

Yet through this death, through his taking on the curse, the forgive-ness of sins was made possible. Jesus Christ offered himself up as the per-fect sacrifice for sins, taking the wrath of God upon himself, and obtaining the forgiveness of sins that the world so desperately needed. But belief in Jesus does not merely wash away previous sins and leave us neutral before God, striving for the rest of our lives to maintain God's favor. This would be tantamount to us needing to earn our salvation through works. Instead, his own perfect record is given to us as a free gift. This is called *imputation*, and just as Adam's guilt was imputed to us, so is Christ's righteousness. Therefore, whoever believes in Jesus is forgiven their sins and receives Christ's perfection as their own. This is what we call *justification*. We are counted as guiltless before the throne of God thanks to Jesus' vicarious atonement forgiving our sins, and because his perfect righteousness is applied to us.

It should be clear that this has huge implications for our present lives as believers. First, even when we do fall into sin, when we come before God and confess, he forgives us because of the work of Christ on the cross. We see this in 1 John 1:9: "If we confess our sins, he is faithful and just and will forgive us our sins and purify us from all unrighteousness." Secondly, we can, with boldness, approach the throne of God in prayer, knowing we have been made righteous before him by being found in Christ. We have had Christ's righteousness imputed to us, giving us the confidence to enter God's presence and enjoy communion with him.

Reflection Questions

1. How much do you contemplate the death of Christ for you?
2. How does knowing that Jesus' perfect record is given to you change the way you see his love?

Prayer

Father, we thank you for your Son Jesus Christ, who gave himself completely for us. We could never walk the walk he walked but he has freely given us his own righteousness. Forgive us when we do not take this seriously enough. Help us to see your great love for us in Jesus Christ. Amen.

DAY 34

Q. What is adoption?

A. Adoption is when we are received into God's family and have a right to all the privileges of the children of God.

For those who are led by the Spirit of God are the children of God. The Spirit you received does not make you slaves, so that you live in fear again; rather, the Spirit you received brought about your adoption to sonship. And by him we cry, "Abba, Father." The Spirit himself testifies with our spirit that we are God's children.

—ROMANS 8:14-16

WHEN SOMEONE PASSES AWAY a part of the process is the reading of the last will and testament. In this ritual, the possessions of the deceased, designated as gifts, are distributed to people. The will, therefore, is a written document composed before their passing, outlining this process in a legally binding way. Generally speaking, these things are distributed to family members, usually sons and daughters, whether biological or adopted. Whoever is written into the will receives the inheritance of the deceased.

In Scripture, this practice is used as an analogy to describe some of the benefits of adoption. Turning to the Bible we see that we too have been adopted into God's family as sons and daughters through Jesus Christ. Therefore, we can be certain that we will receive the promised inheritance he has for us as his sons and daughters. Ephesians 1:11 says, "In him [Jesus Christ] we have obtained an inheritance" (ESV).

Which raises a question: How are we made sons and daughters of God? What accomplished this adoption process? The answer is that all this

68

is made possible through Jesus Christ's death on the cross. In this one act of self-giving love, he made us sons and daughters of God the Father, while at the same time dying the death necessary to make his inheritance ours. We have been written into the will, in a sense, and are guaranteed a promised inheritance as benefactors of that will.

Likewise, as God's adopted sons and daughters, we can call on him as our Father, trusting that he hears us out of his love. We receive Christ as our brother, who intercedes with the Father on our behalf, and the Holy Spirit dwelling in us is "the deposit guaranteeing our inheritance" in Jesus Christ by making God's presence known to us (Eph 1:14). Therefore, let us rejoice as members of God's family who will one day receive a glorious inheritance beyond our wildest imaginations.

Reflection Questions

1. What are some ways that being adopted into God's family can bring you comfort?

2. Does knowing that God is your Father, Christ your brother, and the Holy Spirit the guarantor change the way you view your relationship with them?

Prayer

Merciful and Holy Father, we pray that we might live as your sons and daughters. Help us to show others the same love you have shown to us in Jesus Christ. Fill us with your Holy Spirit so that we can go out in your power and share your love. Amen.

DAY 35

Q. What is sanctification?

A. Sanctification is when we are renewed in the image of God and are enabled more and more to say "no" to sin and "yes" to obedience.

Since, then, you have been raised with Christ, set your hearts on things above, where Christ is seated at the right hand of God. Set your minds on things above, not on earthly things. For you died, and your life is now hidden with Christ in God.

—COLOSSIANS 3:1–3

AFTER GOD WORKS IN our heart by his Holy Spirit, regenerating us and allowing us to accept Jesus Christ as our Lord and Savior, we begin the ongoing process of sanctification. This is the process God uses to grow us in holiness. In some ways we are already sanctified as believers when we are set apart as holy in Jesus Christ's death. Yet, more commonly, sanctification refers to the process by which we walk away from sin and into Christlikeness.

The Bible is clear that we participate in our sanctification as we work to walk away from sin in our lives. First Corinthians 9:25 uses the metaphor of a runner who trains his body physically for a race to describe the work of sanctification in the believer. Philippians 2:12 urges us to "work out your salvation with fear and trembling," as if to say we must teach ourselves to fear the Lord. James argues that faith without accompanying works of obedience is dead (Jas 2:26). From this it should be clear that good works—and growth in good works—is an essential part of the Christian life.

70

On the other hand, our participation in striving to do good works so that we may live more like Christ does not nullify God's grace which he has already bestowed upon us. It does not mean that we somehow earn our way into heaven. Instead, throughout the process of sanctification the Holy Spirit is sustaining and enabling us to walk in the new life we have received from Jesus Christ. It is only through the work of the Holy Spirit in our life that we experience any sort of sanctification. In other words, our growth towards Christlikeness is also a gift of God through the Spirit, and thus an act of God's grace towards us.

Reflection Questions

1. What is sanctification and in what ways are you growing to be more like Christ?
2. How is sanctification an act of God's grace towards us?

Prayer

Father, help us to walk like Christ in everything we do. Fill us with the Holy Spirit so that we can say no to our sin. Help us see new areas of sin we need to walk away from in our lives. Forgive us where we fall short and remind us of your love for us. Amen.

DAY 36

Q. What benefits do we receive from justification, adoption, and sanctification?

A. The benefits we receive from justification, adoption, and sanctification are assurance of God's love for us, peace, joy in the Holy Spirit, and perseverance in belief to the end.

No, in all these things we are more than conquerors through him who loved us. For I am convinced that neither death nor life, neither angels nor demons, neither the present nor the future, nor any powers, neither height nor depth, nor anything else in all creation, will be able to separate us from the love of God that is in Christ Jesus our Lord.

—ROMANS 8:37-39

THE VERY FACT THAT we have been justified by God (forgiven our sins and given Christ's righteousness), adopted as his sons and daughters, and sanctified (continually walking away from sin and becoming more like Christ) should give us a great confidence in the God we worship. All of these things point to his unending love and grace for us. They are a constant reminder of the fact that God has a deep love and affection for us. They bring peace to our restless hearts as we learn to rest in God alone. They fill us with joy as we begin to realize that nothing in this life can separate us from God's love. They remind us that God is for us and that we will persevere in this knowledge till the end of time.

This is not true of people who refuse to believe in Jesus. They can never know with any certainty whether God loves them or if he will judge them as sinners. While most people who don't believe in God do not reflect upon God's love or judgment if the question arises, they are yet unable to quell their disquieted spirits. Similarly, those who are far from God cannot have lasting peace because the things they look for peace in are constantly wasting away. The idols of their hearts never satisfy them, whether it be money, sex, career, intimacy, you name it. They can never experience lasting joy because the pursuit of happiness apart from Christ always ends in failure. For the unbeliever life is a constantly changing, hard-to-understand exercise in futility.

On the other hand, the believer has a firm foundation upon which their life is built, the love of God in Jesus Christ. The Holy Spirit working in their hearts makes present the love of God for them, satisfying their souls and bringing them joy. Here they find rest for their souls and knowledge of an eternity with God that allows them to weather the storms of this life. This is not to say that Christians approach life with a stoic indifference as if they were from the planet Vulcan, devoid of emotional responses. Instead, Christians experience the fullest emotions. Christians experience deep hurt at the sin of the world and deep joy in the love of God. This vacillation between pain and joy reflects how Christ has formed us to see the world. It is a temporary habitation in which we are merely pilgrims.

Reflection Questions

1. After the last few questions-and-answers, do you have a better understanding of God's love for you?

2. How do justification, adoption, and sanctification change the way you see God?

Prayer

Almighty Father, you are the God who justifies the sinner, who adopts people as his own, and who grows them in holiness. Help us, Lord, as we seek to live more into these realities each day. Forgive us when we look elsewhere for the things only you can provide, like assurance, joy, and peace. Give us your grace to face this day in the knowledge of your salvation. Amen.

DAY 37

Q. What benefits do believers receive from Christ
when they die?

A. When believers die, they are made perfect, all sin
is removed, and they immediately go to heaven, where
they dwell with God until the resurrection from the dead.

*Then he said, "Jesus, remember me when you come into your kingdom."
Jesus answered him, "Truly I tell you, today you will be with me in
paradise."*

—LUKE 23:42-43

WHEN TALKING ABOUT WHAT happens after we die, the current cultural consensus appears to be that nothing happens. We merely decompose from a living thing into the disparate elements contained within our bodies. We rot in the ground until we are forgotten, and that's it. Our lives are nothing more than an insignificant historical footnote. It should be no surprise then that this narrative is quickly forgotten when death is a more present reality. All too often people who are quick to challenge the idea of an afterlife comfort those who are mourning with this very idea. Thus, when a philosophical materialist says, "Oh, they're in a better place," they are either liars about their position or morally repugnant counsellors who deceive to avoid uncomfortable truths.

However, we should not be fooled by the narrative that all we are is material substance, and thus, to matter we shall return. Any intellectual position arrogant enough to suggest that for thousands of years prior to its formulation the entirety of the human species was whole-hog wrong should make us suspicious. For millennia, humanity has tended to hold some sort of belief about the afterlife. It has only been very recently that belief in an afterlife has been challenged by the materialistic worldview of the West. It's only been recently that people have begun to believe that nothing exists beyond the observable world.

For Christians, our beliefs regarding the afterlife are informed by Scripture rather than a cultural ideology. Here we find that, upon the death of a believer, they go immediately to be with Christ in heaven. Jesus himself promises this when he says to the thief on the cross, "today you will be with me in paradise" (Luke 23:43). Here the believer remains with Christ until the final resurrection, when he will make all things new. Therefore, life is not pointless struggle and toil until we die and return to the ground. Instead, life has a greater purpose: preparing us for the kingdom of God, where all things are restored to perfection in Jesus Christ.

Reflection Questions

1. What do most of the people in your life think happens after you die?

2. What does the Bible teach about death and what happens after we die?

Prayer

Father, we long for the day when we will be with you in paradise. We long for the day when all things will be made new at the return of Jesus. Lord, we know that this life is not empty and pointless, but is preparing us for the greater glory of heaven. Help us, Lord, by your Spirit, to prepare well. Amen.

Day 38

Q. What benefits do believers receive from Christ at the resurrection?

A. At the resurrection believers are raised up with new bodies and will dwell with God on the new earth for all eternity.

Then I saw "a new heaven and a new earth," for the first heaven and the first earth had passed away, and there was no longer any sea. I saw the Holy City, the new Jerusalem, coming down out of heaven from God, prepared as a bride beautifully dressed for her husband. And I heard a loud voice from the throne saying, "Look! God's dwelling place is now among the people, and he will dwell with them. They will be his people, and God himself will be with them and be their God. He will wipe every tear from their eyes. There will be no more death or mourning or crying or pain, for the old order of things has passed away."

—REVELATION 21:1-4

NO ONE CAN DENY the complete nightmarish gong-show that is the world we inhabit. There is so much evil, so much pain, so much hurt, that to deny the evil we see all around us would be the most absurd blindness one could possibly imagine. Only the completely ignorant or the morally destitute deny the reality of evil. However, despite the pervading presence of evil in the world, it is important to remember that this evil is not eternal. It will be dealt with.

76

One of the most profound passages in Scripture—which speaks to this very issue—can be found at the end of the book of Revelation. In this text our hope for a future that is free of evil is restored. There we are given a glimpse into the final judgment of evil and into the new creation, one where God promises to be "with" us, to "wipe away every tear" from our eyes, and to remove our "mourning" from us forever (Rev 21:3, 4). These are promises which we hunger for like a man bereft of bread. We thirst for them like someone in a desert, far from all bodies of water. We long for their fulfillment with a groaning too deep for words.

All of these promises, promises of judgment and restoration, are fulfilled at the return of Christ. There he will judge the living and the dead and raise up everyone who believes in him to eternal life. Once these things have been accomplished by Christ, he will completely restore the universe, bringing the entirety of creation into perfect harmony. Yet, Christ does not merely set things right, he sets things right so that he might dwell with us. This will be his joy. He wants to walk with us, to talk with us, and to commune with us. This is the ultimate hope of the gospel. When we look to the cross, we see the ultimate picture of God's grace. When we look at the promises of new creation, we see the final outworking of that grace for us.

Reflection Questions

1. Are you excited for Jesus Christ's return?
2. What does it mean to dwell with God for all eternity?

Prayer

Father in heaven, we worship you as the one true God of the universe. You are making all things new through your Son Jesus Christ. We long for the day when everything will be set right. Give us patience as we await that day. Help us to walk in step with the Spirit in our waiting. Amen.

DAY 39

Q. What does God require of people?

A. God requires obedience that comes from faith.

But someone will say, "You have faith; I have deeds." Show me your faith without deeds, and I will show you my faith by my deeds. You believe that there is one God. Good! Even the demons believe that—and shudder. You foolish person, do you want evidence that faith without deeds is useless?

—JAMES 2:18–20

IT'S IMPORTANT TO NOTICE that in our answer today obedience is not left without a qualifying statement. Here we read that God requires obedience that comes from faith. This means that we don't simply muster up our strength, pull up our bootstraps, and obey with all our might. God is not a harsh taskmaster that asks us to make bricks without straw. Rather he gives us what we need to obey. God gives what he demands, meaning that God gives us the gift of faith in him, and as we have faith in Jesus, we are enabled to be obedient to God's will.

Unfortunately, we are prone in our sinfulness to find this concept difficult to understand. We are constantly falling into the temptation to obey God not out of love, but for remuneration. We fall into a trap, acting as if our own strength can bring us salvation. We deceive ourselves by saying, "As long as I am good enough, then God won't judge me." Yet, this ignores and undermines the very nature of the gospel, that it is fully an act of God's free grace. Instead, obedience is made possible through the Holy Spirit's work in us, showing us God's love. And as we experience God's love we are moved to obey.

Think about it like this: When you love someone, you willingly do the things they ask simply because you love them. If a man were only obedient to his wife so that he might earn her affection we would think he is a sociopath. Instead, we expect a husband to listen to his wife and willingly act in obedience because he possesses a deep love for her. This is similar to our relationship with God. When God shows his love for us in Jesus Christ, and makes that love known to us individually through his Holy Spirit, we love him and willingly serve him as a response to that love. In other words, our good works flow from the reality of the gospel. Knowing this frees us from anxiously attempting to earn God's approval.

Reflection Questions

1. What is your heart's motive behind doing good works?
2. What area of your life are you most struggling to obey God in?

Prayer

Father, you love us and have shown your love for us in Jesus Christ. I pray that we might rest in the knowledge that you love us rather than trying to earn your favor. Show us. Lord. where we are trying to earn your favor, and help us repent of this by your Holy Spirit. Fill our hearts with your love so that we too may love. Amen.

DAY 40

Q. What did God give to people to show them what obedience is?

A. God gave people a summary of obedience in the Ten Commandments.

Blessed is the one who does not walk in step with the wicked or stand in the way that sinners take or sit in the company of mockers, but whose delight is in the law of the Lord, and who meditates on his law day and night. That person is like a tree planted by streams of water, which yields its fruit in season and whose leaf does not wither—whatever they do prospers.

—PSALM 1:1–3

THE IDEA THAT GOD has a law for his people—which is irrevocable and must be obeyed for human flourishing—is thought by most to be repressive, tyrannical, and bigoted. For this reason, the Ten Commandments have become less and less influential in the daily lives of most people. They have been replaced with what might be described as *individual autonomy*, where the subject determines for themselves what is right and wrong. The law of self-actualization has replaced the perfect law of God.

Thus, we should be careful that we do not undermine the value of the Ten Commandments by teaching that they no longer apply to the church. God's word is true and valuable, always. It does not become more or less applicable with the changing thoughts of culture. His moral law is irrevocably true no matter the direction the culture goes. This point is extremely important for us in our current cultural climate. Culture is rapidly shifting and changing. Likewise, Western culture is becoming more monolithic as social media spreads Western music, TV shows, memes, and other things to the wider world. The result of this has been an ever-more-powerful narrative of self-actualization and fulfillment which is opposed to any higher moral standard being applied directly to people's lives.

When we look, then, at these important commands of God, we should recognize two things. First, the Ten Commandments are not "rules" to follow that somehow earn us salvation. We are saved by the work of Jesus Christ alone. The Ten Commandments do not overtake or undermine the reality of God's grace. Secondly, just because they don't save us does not mean they are not God's will for our life. When we look at the Ten Commandments, we see a summary of what God desires people to do and be like. They are not merely suggestions that sound pithy and nice but, like all of God's words, they are true, transformative, and powerful. They are fundamental moral realities we all would intuitively understand if it were not for our sin. We as Christians should seek to live lives that conform to God's will. The Ten Commandments reveal that will to us and thus we should seek to be obedient to them as we trust in God's saving grace.

Reflection Questions

1. Do you know the Ten Commandments? If so, what are they?

2. Have you ever been taught that the Ten Commandments are a hindrance to salvation by grace alone?

Prayer

Gracious and merciful God, thank you for the words you have revealed to us in the Ten Commandments. Lord, we are such sinful people and we know that we can never live up to the standard of sinlessness. Yet, you saved us through Jesus Christ and freed us from our attempts to earn our salvation. Help us to live out these commandments not as things that save us, but as things which show us Christlikeness. We pray you would do this through the Holy Spirit. Amen.

Day 41

Q. How can the Ten Commandments be summed up?

A. The Ten Commandments can be summed up in this:
to love the Lord our God with all our heart, soul, mind,
and strength, and to love our neighbors as ourselves.

*Jesus replied: "'Love the Lord your God with all your heart and with
all your soul and with all your mind.' This is the first and greatest commandment. And the second is like it: 'Love your neighbor as yourself.' All
the Law and the Prophets hang on these two commandments."*

—MATTHEW 22:37–40

OFTENTIMES WHEN WE THINK of the Ten Commandments we think of a
list of rules. We think of legal textbooks and courts. Maybe we even think
of the list of household rules our parents had on the refrigerator for us to
always see. Whatever it is that we think of when we hear the words "the Ten
Commandments," chances are that we hear something oppressive rather
than something freeing. Yet, our answer today lays out the purpose of the
Ten Commandments in a much deeper sense than mere rules.

In our answer we learn that the Ten Commandments fundamentally
reveal how God desires for us to love him. As we are obedient to these
commandments, we are showing God that we love him and cherish him
enough to hear his voice and listen to it. The Ten Commandments are not
a list of rules which, if followed perfectly, save us. Rather they are a list of
moral standards which, when obeyed, reveal our love for God. And as we
love God, we necessarily love others because God loves others.

In this we see God's grace. God did not have to give a law to people so that they might live peacefully with God and one another but, out of his grace towards us, he did. Obedience to this law is not an end in itself but is a response to the gracious love of God. This love of God is most fully revealed in Jesus Christ, who died for our sins. And since God showed his great love for us in Jesus we can "love because he first loved us" (1 John 4:19). The Ten Commandments show us more clearly how to love God and love others, which is rooted and grounded in God's love for us as demonstrated in Jesus Christ.

Reflection Questions

1. Do you think of the Ten Commandments as a list of rules which are oppressive and hard to follow?
2. How is God's grace revealed in the Ten Commandments?

Prayer

Father, you not only love us, but you teach us what love looks like. Thank you for the words we find in the Ten Commandments, where we learn to love you and other people. Fill us with the Holy Spirit so we might walk in these things all our lives. Forgive us where we fail and help us trust in your grace. Amen.

Day 42

Q. What is the preface to the Ten Commandments?

A. The preface to the Ten Commandments is this,
"I am the Lord your God, who brought you out of Egypt, out
of the land of slavery" (Exod 20:2).

*Because he loved your ancestors and chose their descendants after them,
he brought you out of Egypt by his Presence and his great strength, to
drive out before you nations greater and stronger than you and to bring
you into their land to give it to you for your inheritance, as it is today.
Acknowledge and take to heart this day that the Lord is God in heaven
above and on the earth below. There is no other. Keep his decrees and
commands, which I am giving you today, so that it may go well with you
and your children after you and that you may live long in the land the
Lord your God gives you for all time.*

—DEUTERONOMY 4:37–40

IMAGINE IF YOU WERE a slave in a foreign country, amongst people you
didn't know, and you were forced to work all day without breaks. Imagine
if you continually endured suffering at the hand of slaveholders who beat
you mercilessly till you lost the will for revolt. But then, someone saved you
from this life and gave you freedom. What would you do? If this were the
lot that you had been dealt in life, and then someone rescued you out of that
life, you would never forget the amazing thing they had done for you. You
would thank them, love them, and be forever grateful.

Similarly, when we look at the Bible, we see this same pattern on repeat. The people are oppressed by an evil force, God saves them, and they are to be eternally grateful. One example of this pattern is God's salvation of Israel from the Egyptians. The Egyptians were horrible slave drivers that mistreated the Israelites for their own personal gain. They even ran a campaign of genocide against Hebrew boys to quell the population growth Israel was experiencing. They were tyrannical megalomaniacs and their cruelty was on a scale we cannot even fathom. Yet, God heard his people's cries and he rescued them out of the hands of the Egyptians. God, in his justice, poured out plagues upon the Egyptians until they recognized God's power and released the Israelites from slavery. For this reason, the Israelites constantly reflected on this event throughout all of Scripture. God's delivery of them from Egypt was the ultimate picture of God's love and kindness towards them.

When we look at the preface to the Ten Commandments, God reminds them of his saving work in freeing them from oppression. He begins the Ten Commandments with a reminder of his grace and love towards them. God's unmerited favor towards them comes before the law that he is about to lay out. This speaks volumes about God's expectation of obedience. It reminds the Israelites that God has already saved them and, therefore, obedience can be the *only* response. His saving them through the exodus is what marks them out as his people, and obedience follows from that. For us, as Christians, our salvation through Jesus marks us out as his people, and our obedience follows from this fact.

Reflection Questions

1. Why was the exodus such an important event in the lives of God's people?

2. Why is it so important that God reminds the Israelites of his grace before he gives them the Ten Commandments?

DAY 42

Prayer

Holy and merciful God, we look to you as the God who saves the oppressed. You heard your people's cries and brought them out of Egypt. You have heard our cries and saved us from a greater slavemaster: sin. Thank you for your Son Jesus, who gave his own life so that ours may be redeemed. Amen.

DAY 43

Q. What does the preface to the Ten Commandments teach us?

A. The preface to the Ten Commandments teaches us that God is the Lord, is our God, and is our Savior.

But he brought his people out like a flock; he led them like sheep through the wilderness. He guided them safely, so they were unafraid; but the sea engulfed their enemies. And so he brought them to the border of his holy land, to the hill country his right hand had taken.

—PSALM 78:52-54

GOD IS ALL-POWERFUL. POWERFUL enough, in fact, to deliver an entire nation from the most ruthless empire of its time, as he did when he rescued Israel from Egypt. He is the Lord almighty, *El Shaddai,* and in his great power he is for us. God is not merely the all-powerful Lord of the universe who is distantly watching but not participating. No, he is *our* God, and he is actively involved in loving care with all of creation.

Now God is not *ours* in the sense of ownership like *our car* or *our home,* but *ours* in the sense of relationship like *our family.* God, despite his power and grandeur, decided to give himself over to relationship with a particular people, Israel, and he became *their* God. Since, this relationship is based on faith he has become *our* God too through belief in Jesus.

Part of this relationship with God is his saving work. Notice again the order which God uses to present himself to the Israelites in the Ten Commandments. He opens with a reminder of how he brought them out of Egypt, his loving grace, and then he gives them commandments outlining what it means to be in relationship to him. God's gracious love and self-giving relationship come before the law.

We see this gracious love on full display in Jesus Christ, who gave himself up on the cross to redeem humanity from their sins. He reveals God's gracious love toward us, and his salvation comes to us apart from anything we do or have done. It is only after this salvation comes to us that we can live into the new life, by the Holy Spirit, of loving God and loving others. It was true for the Israelites and it is true for us.

Reflection Questions

1. Why is the order of which comes first, rescue or obedience, so important?

2. How is Jesus the ultimate picture of God's self-giving love?

Prayer

Father, you are Lord, you are God, and you are our Savior. We look to Jesus as the one who saves us from our sins and reveals your love to us. Forgive us when we think we can earn our salvation, and lead us into your mercy. Amen.

DAY 44

Q. What is the first commandment?

A. The first commandment is to have no other gods.

You shall have no other gods before me.

—EXODUS 20:3

THERE IS ONE TRUE God who was before all things and who is the maker of all things. This God has been revealed to us in the Scriptures and, because he revealed himself to us in the Scriptures, to even talk of other gods is simply absurd. There can only be one all-powerful, all-knowing, creative being. If anything in the universe had a résumé which challenged Yahweh's then we would be unable to call him God. He would automatically become impotent and unable to act the way we once thought. Simply put, nothing can measure up to God because he is beyond compare. Everything else is merely a fantasy or demonic.

Yet, human beings have a tendency to make up and worship other gods because our sinfulness has distorted us to the point where we actively seek to abandon the one true God. This is something that is displayed in Scripture when it talks of idolatry. We are even given a frightening picture of the Israelites—who have just been led through the Red Sea—caving into their idolatrous impulses at Mount Horeb by creating a golden calf (Exod 32:1–6). If people who have seen God's glory, seen his mighty works, seen his destruction of a nation, can fall into idolatry, then it, without doubt, is the most ingrained sin of the human heart.

The New Testament writers acknowledge this as well. Paul writes in Romans 1:21, "For although they knew God, they neither glorified him as

God nor gave thanks to him, but their thinking became futile and their foolish hearts were darkened." Sin has so blinded people's minds that they exchange the knowledge of the one true God in order to worship a "human being," "birds," "animals," and "reptiles" (Rom 1:23). Truly the human heart is the greatest mass-producer of idols.

Despite this atrocious sin of idolatry, God became man in the person of Jesus Christ to atone for our sin and restore us to right relationship with him. And as the promised Holy Spirit dwells in our hearts, making God known to us, we can worship God alone in the knowledge that we have been saved through Jesus Christ. We are freed from our idol production and can now look to the one true God.

Reflection Questions

1. Why are humans so prone to worship things other than the one true God?

2. Have you ever thought about other gods as either fantasy or demonic?

Prayer

Father, Son, and Spirit, you alone are the God of the universe. We worship you and praise you for the great works you have done. Thank you for the death of the Son, Jesus Christ, so that we might be forgiven. Help us by the Holy Spirit to worship you alone. Amen.

DAY 45

Q. What is required of us in the first commandment?

A. The first commandment requires us to acknowledge God to be the only true God and to worship and glorify him.

All who make idols are nothing, and the things they treasure are worthless. Those who would speak up for them are blind; they are ignorant, to their own shame. Who shapes a god and casts an idol, which can profit nothing? People who do that will be put to shame. Such craftsmen are only human beings. Let them all come together and take their stand; they will be brought down to terror and shame.

—ISAIAH 44:9-11

WHY IS THE GOD of the Bible such a jealous God? Why is he so concerned with everyone, everywhere, giving him praise, honor, and glory? Why is he so opposed to people worshiping objects of wood and stone even if these things are meant to represent him? Why is it that people are required to worship him alone and not some other god? These are valid questions and they have been asked time and time again by thinkers throughout the centuries, attempting to undercut the Christian faith.

However, when we understand who the God of the Bible really is then praising him alone is the only option. God is not merely one god among others, but he is *the* God. He alone created the universe and he alone sustains it with his word of power. He is above all things, beyond all things, and before all things. Nothing is worthy of praise and honor besides him. Thus, God is a jealous God because he alone is worthy of worship.

There is another reason, however, why the worship of God alone is so important. Because what we worship shapes who we are as people. If we worship the wrong things, then inevitably, we are shaped by something other than the source of all goodness; God himself. If we are shaped by something other than the source of all goodness then the result will be moral chaos. This is precisely what happened every time the Israelites turned away from worshiping God. They began practicing evil and fell into the chaos that ensues when one bows down to created things. Thanks be to God for Jesus Christ, our Savior, who redeemed us out of our sin and, by the Holy Spirit, allows us to worship God alone.

Reflection Questions

1. What does it mean that God is jealous?
2. Why does God demand we worship him alone?

Prayer

Heavenly Father, help us to worship you alone. Forgive us where we look to other things for the provision only you can give. Lead us, Lord, into the life everlasting that is found in Jesus alone. Amen.

Day 46

Q. What is forbidden in the first commandment?

A. The first commandment forbids denying, not worshiping, or not glorifying the true God as God. It also forbids worshiping any other thing as God.

We know that we are children of God, and that the whole world is under the control of the evil one. We know also that the Son of God has come and has given us understanding, so that we may know him who is true. And we are in him who is true by being in his Son Jesus Christ. He is the true God and eternal life. Dear children, keep yourselves from idols.

—1 JOHN 5:19-21

MY GUESS IS THAT when we think of the first commandment, we think we are doing a pretty good job at it. Most of us don't have shrines to other gods in our homes which we bow down to whenever the harvest is particularly bad. Most of us don't head into the local temple dedicated to other deities and bow down to those pseudo-gods, asking for fertility or wealth. So we think that we keep this commandment quite easily. Yet, the first commandment goes much deeper than a superficial understanding of other gods.

Our hearts tend to look to a plethora of other things for that which only God can provide. We look for security in finances, we look for approval in our looks, we seek satisfaction and happiness in drugs, alcohol, and sex. All in all, people are really good at looking to things other than God to provide what only God can. We have an almost infinite capacity to search for happiness and fulfillment in wrong-headed pursuits. Yet, this is precisely what the first commandment forbids us to do.

Furthermore, we should never be so naïve as to think we are perfectly obedient to this law or free from the temptation of idolatry. Each and every one of us does this and we all fall short of the first commandment. But in this the grace of God is revealed to us. We are not saved through obedience to this commandment, but through the atoning death of Jesus Christ on the cross. Thus, it's as we look to him and experience the transforming work of the Holy Spirit in our hearts that we can begin to practice obedience to this commandment. It is only as our allegiance is shifted by the Holy Spirt, towards Jesus Christ and God the Father, that we can begin to walk away from idolatry. It's only in Jesus that the idol factory in the human heart is completely shut down.

Reflection Questions

1. What do you look to for security; comfort, happiness, or satisfaction?

2. Do you rest in the grace of God—revealed in Jesus Christ—or do you try to earn your salvation?

Prayer

Gracious Father, we look to you as the God who loves us. Thank you for creating and sustaining us. Forgive us for looking towards other things to provide what only you can. Nothing can satisfy our hearts but you. Help us, Lord, to trust in you for everything we need. Amen.

Day 47

Q. What is the second commandment?

A. The second commandment is to not make any images for the purpose of worship.

You shall not make for yourself an image in the form of anything in heaven above or on the earth beneath or in the waters below. You shall not bow down to them or worship them; for I, the Lord your God, am a jealous God, punishing the children for the sin of the parents to the third and fourth generation of those who hate me, but showing love to a thousand generations of those who love me and keep my commandments.

—EXODUS 20:4-6

THE FIRST COMMANDMENT IS that, generally speaking, we must worship God alone. The second commandment, on the other hand, focuses on images. The great irony here is that as God was giving these commandments to Moses, the Israelites were busy breaking this very command. They took off their gold jewelry, melted it down, and molded it into a calf, with their priest declaring, "These are your gods, Israel, who brought you up out of Egypt" (Exod 32:4). They had fallen into sin and turned immediately towards idolatry.

Now, in fairness, some people argue that they were attempting to create a representation of God himself. If this were the case then the intention behind their actions may have been good. We can't know for certain their hearts' motive behind creating this image. Yet, even if this were the case, they clearly missed the mark and fell into horrendous sin. God is so above human comprehension that any attempt to create a likeness of him fails to capture his essence. In fact, any attempt to create an image of God Almighty distorts who he truly is.

This commandment is an outright ban on the production of any image attempting to represent the Lord. Even religious art can never capture God's nature and, therefore, is prone to distort who he is. The artist applies to God characteristics which are nothing but the fanciful imaginations of his own mind. No physical representation can capture his strength, or his love, or his grace, and any attempt to capture it lacks God's true nature by limiting the unlimitable. Hence, God commands that no images of any kind be made for the purposes of worship because, when they are used, what is being worshiped is not God as he has revealed himself to us in Scripture.

Reflection Questions

1. What false images of God do we worship?
2. Why are images so dangerous to our worship of God?

Prayer

Merciful and wonderful God, nothing can capture your great majesty. You are above every conception we have of you. Forgive us for the images we create to contain you. Lead us by the Holy Spirit into a deeper understanding of who you are through your word. Amen.

DAY 48

Q. What is required of us in the second commandment?

A. The second commandment requires us to worship God as he has revealed himself to us.

The Son is the image of the invisible God, the firstborn over all creation. For in him all things were created: things in heaven and on earth, visible and invisible, whether thrones or powers or rulers or authorities; all things have been created through him and for him. He is before all things, and in him all things hold together.

—COLOSSIANS 1:15–17

GOD IS ABOVE EVERY conception we could ever dream up regarding him. He is so much greater than our perception allows us to grasp that we will never have a complete understanding of God. Our understanding of God will always be incomplete. God is the holy infinite Creator and we are the finite lowly creature. Nothing we can do will ever allow us to climb up to God. We can't reason our way up to him through sheer speculation and imagination. Which puts us in a predicament, that is, "How do we know God?"

Well, in order for us to know God he has to reveal himself to us. And the way God chose to reveal himself to us is not in paintings, images, or idols, but through his own word. God acted in human history, performed miraculous deeds, and led particular men to record these events in the holy Scriptures by his Holy Spirit. This is why we can say that our knowledge of God is incomplete, but not deficient. It is incomplete because God is infinite, but it is still sufficient because in God's word we have all of the knowledge deemed necessary for us by God.

Additionally, in Scripture we find the story of God's unending love for humanity as he works to bring about their redemption through his son Jesus. He is the person who reveals the nature of God more than anything else. In Jesus we see the love of God on full display as he gives himself up on the cross so that humanity might be saved through him. In Jesus we see the wrath of God fulfilled as sin is fully punished on the cross. In Jesus we see the power of God as he rises from the dead, defeating death. It's only as we look to Jesus that we see the full revelation of God for us. We don't get to pick and choose what is revealed to us, but God reveals himself to us as he pleases. This he did in Jesus Christ, and he makes him known to us through his word.

Reflection Questions

1. Why must we worship God as he has revealed himself to us?

2. What does it mean that our knowledge of God is incomplete but not deficient?

Prayer

Lord, you have revealed yourself to us most fully in the person and work of Jesus Christ. We look to him and the testimony we find regarding him all throughout Scripture. Father, help us to destroy misconceptions we have of you and build us up by your word. Amen.

DAY 49

Q. What is forbidden in the second commandment?

A. The second commandment forbids us to worship anything manmade, including our own ideas.

Aaron answered them, "Take off the gold earrings that your wives, your sons and your daughters are wearing, and bring them to me." So all the people took off their earrings and brought them to Aaron. He took what they handed him and made it into an idol cast in the shape of a calf, fashioning it with a tool. Then they said, "These are your gods, Israel, who brought you up out of Egypt."

—EXODUS 32:2–4

AFTER THE ISRAELITES CREATED the golden calf, Moses came down from the mountain in such a rage that he threw the stone tablets God had written on to the ground, smashing them to pieces. He took the golden calf, pulverized it into dust, and made the Israelites drink to the lees the water with the dust of the idol in it. This is an intense story, and perhaps it seems like an overreaction on the part of Moses. In fact, we may read this story in our Bibles and think that Moses acted in sin because his anger seems so out of proportion to our common sense. Yet, this misses the point of the story.

If anything, the point of this story is to show us the seriousness of the Israelites' crime against God: they defaced his glory through the image they created. Likewise, whenever we create an image of God it's a distortion and misrepresentation of him. It is tainted by our own sinfulness, which can never perceive God in his fullness. Images are dangerous because they give us ideas of God that are not true of his character. Therefore, idols, images, and false representations of God need to be ground down to a fine dust and completely destroyed.

This prohibition even applies to our own thoughts about God. Whenever we construct an image of God in our minds—rather than rely on his word and how he has revealed himself to us—we distort who he is and miss out on the beautiful picture of his character that we find in Scripture. A picture of love, mercy, grace, and patience towards all humanity. A picture of justice, wrath, and righteousness. There is no image, made by human hands or human minds, that can compare with this God. He is perfect in every way and his love is beyond our wildest imaginations.

Reflection Questions

1. In what ways are you thinking falsely about God?

2. Do you create images of God (with your hands or your head) that distort his character?

Prayer

Heavenly Father, you have revealed yourself to us in Jesus, and we find him in your holy word, the Bible. Help us to grow in a more accurate understanding of who you are through Scripture. Forgive us where we fail, and thank you for the love and mercy you have shown us on the cross. Amen.

DAY 50

Q. What is the third commandment?

A. The third commandment is not to misuse the Lord's name.

You shall not misuse the name of the Lord your God, for the Lord will not hold anyone guiltless who misuses his name.

—EXODUS 20:7

LONG AGO THE NATION of Israel was enslaved in the land of Egypt and forced to participate in back-breaking labor. Yet, because of their great cries for help, the Lord came to rescue them out of slavery and deliver them from the hand of the oppressor. He chose Moses from among the people to be his prophet and revealed himself to him through a burning bush. There, at the burning bush, God revealed himself to Moses as, "I AM WHO I AM," and told him his personal name "Yahweh" (Exod 3:14–15).

While this story may not seem like a big deal it is important that we realize the significance of God giving his personal name to Moses. Naming always reveals something about the named. It is the lowest common denominator of description. Unfortunately, we have lost the tendency to fill the names we give to our children with meaning. Yet throughout history this was not the case. Names generally had meaning attached to them. This was even truer for ancient Israel, where names had significance beyond just a designation. They had meaning that extended to previous generations and meaning that pointed to promises of God. For Israelites, naming was significant.

Therefore, God naming himself reveals a significant amount of information regarding the God the Israelites worshiped. It was a revelation of who he was *in himself*, a revelation of God's nature. For this reason, the ancient Israelites held the name of Yahweh in the highest esteem. It was held in such high esteem that when Jewish speakers wished to say Yahweh, they would use a different Hebrew word for God in order to show reverence and respect for the name's greatness. To be cavalier with the name of God, therefore, is to be cavalier with worship to God. Thus, we begin to understand the reasoning behind the third commandment. We begin to see that God's name is worthy of respect.

Reflection Questions

1. Why did Israelites hold the name of God in such high regard?
2. Does knowing the importance of God's name help us understand the third commandment?

Prayer

Holy God, thank you for revealing yourself to us in Scripture. We pray that we might honor your name and that you might forgive us where we have not shown it the respect it deserves. Thank you for your forgiving love and grace. Amen.

Day 51

Q. What is required of us in the third commandment?

A. The third commandment requires a good use of God's names, titles, and attributes.

I will make known my holy name among my people Israel. I will no longer let my holy name be profaned, and the nations will know that I the Lord am the Holy One in Israel. It is coming! It will surely take place, declares the Sovereign Lord. This is the day I have spoken of.

—EZEKIEL 39:7-8

WHEN WE MISUSE THE Lord's name, we are not only being disrespectful to the Creator of the universe, but we are communicating something about him that is untrue. A misuse of his name disparages his reputation as the God who is worthy of worship and praise, which is why the third commandment applies equally to the titles of God and his attributes. When we get these things wrong, we deviate from what Scripture teaches about God, and we inevitably say something that distorts God's character.

It is no wonder that so many misconceptions have sprung up surrounding who God is; they do not take the names, titles, and attributes God reveals about himself seriously. When we look at Scripture, we see a God who is merciful, gracious, abounding in steadfast love, slow to anger, faithful, and just. If we take any of these self-designated attributes less or more seriously than the others, we will, without a doubt, believe in a god different than the God of the Bible. This is because God is indivisible, meaning that he is simple in essence. He cannot be divided into constituent parts. We cannot create a pie chart of God's attributes, dividing them up into percentages we deem good so that God is 75 percent gracious, 10 percent just, and 15 percent merciful. Due to God's simplicity this all-too-common practice is heterodox.

Luckily, we can avoid these pernicious errors by looking to God's most clear revelation of himself, the person and work of Jesus Christ. In him we see demonstrated the perfect love of God through his self-sacrificial death. Romans 5:8 says, "But God demonstrates his own love for us in this: while we were still sinners, Christ died for us," teaching us God's fundamental nature of love. The fact that God is a God of love is not showing us one attribute among many, but is showing us the whole of God's nature, which permeates and informs every attribute ascribed to God. Therefore, we need to be cautious how we speak of God. If we do not take his name, titles, and attributes seriously we will distort who he is and veil the glorious nature of his Son Jesus with a twisted reality.

Reflection Questions

1. Why is it so important that we speak rightly about who God is?
2. How does Jesus reveal God's love for us?

Prayer

Father in Heaven, we worship you alone as the God of the universe. Help us to keep your name pure on our lips. Forgive us where we misstep and distort who you are. Give us your grace. Amen.

Day 52

Q. What is forbidden in the third commandment?

A. The third commandment forbids all misuse of God's names, titles, and attributes.

Take the blasphemer outside the camp. All those who heard him are to lay their hands on his head, and the entire assembly is to stone him. Say to the Israelites: "Anyone who curses their God will be held responsible; anyone who blasphemes the name of the Lord is to be put to death. The entire assembly must stone them. Whether foreigner or native-born, when they blaspheme the Name they are to be put to death."

—LEVITICUS 24:14-16

THERE IS NO DOUBT we will fail to keep this commandment. Just like all the rest of the commandments, we will actively fail, and passively fail, at misusing the holy name of God. Even if we don't realize it now, as we grow in our faith and come to know Jesus in a deeper way, we will look back on our lives, realizing that the way we previously thought of God and spoke of him distorted his character. We will fail at being obedient to this commandment simply because we are human. Stuck in sin, blown around by every cultural tide and shifting view, we inevitably will think wrongly of God at some point.

However, we need to be reminded that even when we fail to keep this commandment, God's forgiving love in Jesus Christ saves us out of our sinful state and declares us righteous. While these commandments remind us what it is that God desires from us, they do not save us. We can't somehow keep them perfectly, even if we wanted to, and earn our way into heaven. Paul speaks to this when he argues that "a person is not justified by the works of the law but by faith" (Gal 2:16). People are justified by Christ through faith and redeemed from the "curse" of the law, as Paul goes on to say: "Christ redeemed us from the curse of the law by becoming a curse for us" (Gal 3:13). Therefore, we rest in God's unmerited favor towards us. We abide in the free gift of grace which comes through the work of Jesus Christ.

Our keeping the commandments will always be a mixed bag of obedience and failure, but the hope of salvation doesn't rest on obedience or failure. Failure is highly discouraged, and obedience is highly encouraged. Disobedience needs to be punished and obedience is rewarded. Yet, not because they earn God's redemption, but because both obedience and failure say something about our love for God. As Christians we don't fear for our salvation every time we fall into temptation. Instead, we rest assured that nothing can separate us from the love of God in Jesus Christ who bore the punishment for our disobedience on the cross.

Reflection Questions

1. What does obedience to the Ten Commandments say about your relationship with God?

2. In what ways have you failed to keep the third commandment, and have you sought repentance?

Prayer

Merciful God, we rest on your unfailing love for us. We are not able to keep your commands perfectly, but we rest in the grace of Jesus Christ. Give us tongues that honor your holy name. Let us follow you and look to you always. Empower us by your Spirit. Amen.

Day 53

Q. What is the fourth commandment?

A. The fourth commandment is to keep the Sabbath.

Remember the Sabbath day by keeping it holy. Six days you shall labor and do all your work, but the seventh day is a Sabbath to the Lord your God. On it you shall not do any work, neither you, nor your Son or daughter, nor your male or female servant, nor your animals, nor any foreigner residing in your towns. For in six days the Lord made the heavens and the earth, the sea, and all that is in them, but he rested on the seventh day. Therefore the Lord blessed the Sabbath day and made it holy.

—EXODUS 20:8–11

WE LIVE IN A busy culture, powered by the engine of technological achievements that only make us more busy and more distracted. Donald Bloesch, in his book *Holy Scripture*, presciently points out the results of a growing dependence on technology:

> What dominates the technological society is noise or chatter rather than either the silence of mysticism or the interpreting speech of prophetic religion. Technological planners and social engineers cherish the productivity of human labor more than the understanding of human existence. They gauge human progress on the basis of desired results rather than insight into ultimate reality.[*]

*Bloesch, *Holy Scripture*, 292.

In other words, people who are productive are more valuable than people who are pensive in a technocratic world. Thus, when we aren't endlessly striving towards achievements at school, in sports, or at work, we are endlessly striving for acceptance and connection within a digital world.

Unfortunately, this hodgepodge of activity has made rest such an elusive idea that we do not even know how to rest anymore, and I daresay we don't know what it is either. Yet when we look at the Bible, we find the God who sustains the entirety of the universe, resting on the seventh day of creation. He is the God who governs every moment sustaining all creation, but he is also the God of rest. We read, "Thus the heavens and the earth were completed in all their vast array. By the seventh day God had finished the work he had been doing; so on the seventh day he rested from all his work" (Gen 2:1–2). God quite literally rested from the work of creation, and in this, established rest as a fundamental reality of the universe.

God designed us to find rest and to find joy in our resting; which is precisely why it is so hard. Our sinfulness fights to cause us to act in wrong ways, but it also fights to have us act at the wrong times. Therefore, God commanded us to keep the Sabbath, to rest from our constant work, trusting in God as provider and sustainer of our lives. In today's world we are in desperate need of this rest. We need the rest that God gives to us through the Holy Spirit, freeing us from the shackles of *the pursuit of happiness*. No doubt this commandment applies to a physical time of rest, but we also need rest for our anxious and weary souls. Here we look to Jesus as the one who gives us rest by gifting us with eternal bliss.

Reflection Questions

1. What in your life are you striving for that steals the rest of your soul?
2. How does belief in Jesus free us from a need to strive without rest?

Prayer

Almighty Father, you are the God of rest. We rest in you and trust in your Son, Jesus Christ, for our rest. Free us from the things that prevent us from resting in you and allow us to rest assured of your care and provision. Amen.

DAY 54

Q. What is required of us in the fourth commandment?

A. The fourth commandment requires us to keep a day holy during the week for the purpose of rest.

Thus the heavens and the earth were completed in all their vast array. By the seventh day God had finished the work he had been doing; so on the seventh day he rested from all his work. Then God blessed the seventh day and made it holy, because on it he rested from all the work of creating that he had done.

—GENESIS 2:1-3

NOT LONG AGO IN Western culture it was the norm for businesses to close, activities to cease, and people to stay close to home on Sundays. People saw Sunday as a holy day to the Lord, where rest from activity was meant to take place in conjunction with worship in the church. This strict Sabbatarianism is now practiced only by select denominations and businesses. In fact, the only business I can think of which takes a hard stance on practicing Sabbath sells fried chicken.

The reason I bring this up is because it reveals how far in the other direction the Western world has gone. In our time, everything and everyone is *on* all the time. Even if you leave the office early the office remains in your front pant pocket, constantly buzzing. Emails, texts, social media, and other technological advancements—which were meant to make our lives easier—have created a world of self-imposed slavery where a little black box steals the joy of rest and, furthermore, our mental health. Thus, rest and Sabbath are rarely practiced at all anymore and this certainly has detrimental effects on us as human beings who are created in God's image, people created for the rest of God.

While Scripture has little to say on the specific day Sabbath rest should take place it has lots to say on the Sabbath in general. We are designed for both work and rest. Not rest as we might think of it, like watching TV and playing video games—these things are merely passive modes of escapism. Rather, we were created for active rest. Rest where we seek out God, trust in his provision, and look to him as our Savior and Lord. It's a weekly time of focusing on God and what he has accomplished for our sake in Jesus Christ. This is what is required of us in the fourth commandment; we are to set our sights on Jesus Christ as the one who gives us rest through his life, death, and resurrection and we are to do so in an intentional way for a period of time. It is as we drink from the fullness of God's love, most clearly seen in Jesus Christ and revealed to us by the Holy Spirit, that we learn rest.

Reflection Questions

1. In what ways are you always on and how can you turn off?
2. What does it mean to actively rest and what are some ways you can do that?

Prayer

Father, thank you for your Son Jesus, who has paid the price of our redemption on the cross, and with it bought our rest. Reveal your love to us as we rest in Jesus Christ through the Holy Spirit. Amen.

DAY 55

Q. What is forbidden in the fourth commandment?

A. The fourth commandment forbids being lazy and doing no work, as well as being consumed by work and not resting.

The Pharisees said to him, "Look, why are they doing what is unlawful on the Sabbath?" He answered, "Have you never read what David did when he and his companions were hungry and in need? In the days of Abiathar the high priest, he entered the house of God and ate the consecrated bread, which is lawful only for priests to eat. And he also gave some to his companions." Then he said to them, "The Sabbath was made for man, not man for the Sabbath.

—MARK 2:24–27

TWO THINGS ARE FORBIDDEN in the fourth commandment, both of which we need to be careful of falling into. First, the fourth commandment forbids laziness. This is more than simply not working, it is having no *telos*, no purpose. Laziness is a purposeless drifting in life that exudes nihilistic thought patterns, robbing reality of all meaning. Laziness is a willful scorning of the tasks to which God has called you in order to pursue purposeless pleasures. It is a burying of talents and adding nothing to what has been given to you.

Not only is this sinful, but living in this way is a tragedy. We have been created by God with intentionality and have been bestowed with purpose by God. Think back to the question-and-answer from day one in this devotional. There you will see the purpose for which you were created. Our lives are meant to glorify God and to enjoy the benefits of relationship with him. Therefore, we are not to squander the natural gifts and abilities God has given us so that we might "rest." Not a biblical rest, but a worldly over-indulgence of purposeless rest.

Secondly, the fourth commandment forbids workaholism. This happens when we are consumed with what we do to the point where we find the whole of our identity in our work. We become one with the machine of productivity, no longer seeing ourselves as human beings with multi-dimensional relationships and connections, but rather cogs in a machine that sputters and whirs on the fuel of self-sacrifice for the sake of the global economy. The market never sleeps, thus, you mustn't either. Yet what we do does not define us, but rather our status as forgiven sons and daughters of God through Jesus Christ does.

If we move toward either of these two extremes then we are breaking the fourth commandment and walking in sin. Rather, God desires us to rely completely on him in both our rest and our work. We are meant to rest from a place of purpose, trusting God to give us the rest we need so we may work another day. Similarly, we work from a place of having a secure identity in Christ, trusting God with our work while we rest in him. This is his desire for us, and its fulfillment is found in Jesus Christ, who forgives us our sin and allows us to rest, physically and spiritually, in the knowledge of the love of God.

Reflection Questions

1. Why is either extreme—too much rest or too much work—dangerous?

2. How has Jesus made it so that we can rest and work the way God intended us to?

Prayer

Father, we pray that we might not toil endlessly to achieve things only you can give. We pray that we might not rest in laziness and squander the gifts you have given us. Help us, Holy Spirit, to rest and work well. Amen.

DAY 56

Q. What is the fifth commandment?

A. The fifth commandment is to honor your parents.

Honor your father and your mother, so that you may live long in the land the Lord your God is giving you.

—EXODUS 20:12

THE PARENT-CHILD RELATIONSHIP—APART FROM the relationship between and husband and wife—is one of the most extraordinary relationships that we share in life. Parents shape us and mold us with patterns and habits which effect the entirety of our lives. From its earliest moments the relationship between parent and child has a deep psychological effect on both parties involved. There is no denying that all parents and all children are affected in dramatic ways by the relationship they have to one another.

This should not surprise us given the significance that Scripture gives to this unique relationship. All over Scripture we see the wise advice of parents to their children. We see the dramatic negative effects of parental sin on the lives of children, leaving them with a legacy of brokenness. We are shown examples of fatherhood and motherhood that we are intended to emulate in our own relationships with our children. We are even told in books like Deuteronomy to teach our children God's word. Moses admonishes the Israelites to, "Teach [God's commandments] to your children, talking about them when you sit at home and when you walk along the road" (Deut 11:19).

Yet most profoundly, the relationship between parent and child is the way God chooses to relate to us in Scripture. God is called the "father of the fatherless" (Ps 68:5). He's said to have "compassion on his children" like a father (Ps 103:13). God is said to be like a mother hen who gathers her chicks under her wings for protection (Matt 23:37). All in all, God has revealed himself as our heavenly Father, the eternal representation of true parental love.

From this we should learn the necessity of honoring one's parents. God himself has instituted this relationship for growth, maturity, and sanctification (learning to be more like Christ). He has seen fit to use earthly parents to point us to his fatherly affections. He uses good parents to show children a picture of his love and care for them. Likewise, he uses bad parents to draw the abused to himself as the supreme parent of love who never mistreats his children. Therefore, we are to honor our parents as they perform this God-given duty.

Reflection Questions

1. When God is called our heavenly Father how do you react?
2. How can you find comfort in knowing that God is our heavenly Father?

Prayer

Lord God, thank you for revealing yourself to us as our Father in heaven. We are so grateful for the grace you have shown us in Jesus Christ so that we might be made your sons and daughters. Help us where we dishonor our parents, and forgive us our sins. Amen.

DAY 57

Q. What is required of us in the fifth commandment?

A. The fifth commandment requires us to honor
our parents by submitting to their authority and loving them as
our heavenly Father loves us.

*Children, obey your parents in the Lord, for this is right. "Honor your
father and mother"—which is the first commandment with a promise—
"so that it may go well with you and that you may enjoy long life on the
earth."*

—EPHESIANS 6:1–3

"SUBMISSION" AND "AUTHORITY" ARE dirty words in our society. In some
ways it is more offensive to suggest that someone should be submissive than
it is to verbally assault them with vulgar language. We hate the idea of being under someone else's authority. Freedom in work, life, and society is
increasingly being defined as the removal of authority and subsequently
the removal or our need to submit to those authorities. The underlying
assumption under this thinking is that people are basically good, and therefore they can, more or less, function in society without any authority; they
will naturally do what is right.

Sadly, this is not the case. We are all marred by the devastating effects
of sin, which damage our relationships and allow for things like crime and
division. Jeremiah teaches that, "the heart is deceitful above all things" (Jer
17:9). Our wicked hearts lie and lead us into all sorts of violent conflicts
within ourselves and with others. We need sin to be bridled, not given free
rein.

Because of this, God, in his wisdom, has placed people in relationships of authority and submission to curtail the infectious spread of sin and to keep it in check when it breaks out. This is an act of God's common grace towards all peoples, specifically to prevent the wanton sinfulness that would result if he did not restrain it. One of the relationships God has ordained for this purpose is that of the parent to the child. God designed the universe so that parental love teaches children to decrease sinfulness by showing children what it means to love God and serve him. Therefore, we are in a position of submission to our parents as we submit to God.

Reflection Questions

1. What emotional response do you have to the words "submission" and "authority?"

2. Why are authority and submission necessary in the world?

Prayer

Father, we pray that as we learn to humble ourselves by submitting to you that we might learn to submit to our parents as well. Let us honor them and revere them by loving them. Help us do this, Holy Spirit, and awaken our hearts to your parental love for us. Amen.

Day 58

Q. What is forbidden in the fifth commandment?

A. The fifth commandment forbids dishonoring our parents by not submitting to their authority in the same way we submit to God's authority.

They have become filled with every kind of wickedness, evil, greed and depravity. They are full of envy, murder, strife, deceit and malice. They are gossips, slanderers, God-haters, insolent, arrogant and boastful; they invent ways of doing evil; they disobey their parents; they have no understanding, no fidelity, no love, no mercy.

—ROMANS 1:29-31

IF FREEDOM IS DEFINED as not submitting to anyone's authority, then keeping the fifth commandment becomes an impossibility. When freedom is seen as the ability to choose for oneself any option before one's eyes, people are left unfettered and aimless. Unfortunately, this definition of freedom is becoming more common. This definition is a lie that inevitably leads to more sin and more chaos, which is already being seen in the wider culture. Tolerance for the sake of protecting freedom of this type is slowly eroding our moral foundations and one day the building will collapse. There is no longer any standard by which someone's actions can be judged. This has even permeated into the home, making it so the parents feel unable to discipline and children unwilling to listen. Neither party sees any good in the authority-submission relationship.

Submission and authority need to be reclaimed if any moral fabric is to be maintained. In Scripture, the authority of the parents and the submission of the children is assumed. While we all get frustrated at our parents using their authority in an unfair way, that is no reason to assume that they are never right nor a reason to think that all authority is wrong, nor that our submission to that authority is not required. Unless our parents are asking us to submit to them in a way that would call into question our submission to God's own authority then we are called to submit to them as an act of obedience to God. The fifth commandment forbids the dishonoring of our parents and we need to learn to be okay with this.

However, it's also important to recognize that people are sinners, including our parents. Sometimes, tragically, they sin to such a degree that children experience things they never should have to go through. Sometimes the damage done—emotionally, psychologically, and even physically—seems to be irreparable. But where our earthly parents fail our heavenly Father overcomes. Here we need to be reminded that the God of the universe has shown his love for us in dying for our sins in the person of Jesus Christ. And through this death he makes you his son or daughter by faith. Where your parents have failed, he has succeeded in his never-ending love.

Reflection Questions

1. What is your reaction to the idea that you must be under the authority of your parents?

2. Why is it so important to know that God is our loving Father through faith in Jesus?

Prayer

Heavenly Father, thank you for succeeding where our parents have failed to love us. Forgive us when we dishonor the people you have put into our lives as family. Give us the courage to love them as we have been loved by you. You are the almighty, all-wonderful, all-powerful Father. Thank you. Amen.

Day 59

Q. What is the sixth commandment?

A. The sixth commandment is to not murder.

You shall not murder.

—EXODUS 20:13

THIS COMMANDMENT SEEMS SO obvious to us that it's almost ridiculous that it even needs to be said. We look at it and go, "Well, duh!" But the sad reality is that despite it being obvious, murder happens all the time. People are vindictive, angry, resentful, vengeful sinners capable of the most horrific crimes imaginable because of the sinfulness of the human heart. In fact, many people act in atrocious ways precisely because they are under the impression that they are performing a good deed. The darkness which envelops the sinful mind so dumbfounds people that they become locked in a stupor from which they cannot escape—the stupor of ideology—and this makes them capable of justifying even the most horrendous of actions.

So, before we brush this commandment off as being ridiculous or obvious let's acknowledge our own sinfulness and propensity to sin in ways that we didn't think possible. Let's acknowledge we are not above falling into this sin and breaking this commandment, no matter who we are. Let's be reminded that our sinfulness is the very thing that led to the most horrific murder in history: the death of Jesus Christ.

In his death we see the completely innocent Son of God condemned to death by a crowd of religious Jews who probably saw themselves as decent people, just like us. We see him strung up on a cross, nails pierced through his wrists by Roman soldiers who probably thought they were just doing their job. We see him mocked, scorned, and ridiculed by onlookers who probably thought they were speaking righteously against some criminal. All of these normal people—religious Jews, Roman soldiers, average citizens—complicit in the murder of the Son of God. They killed the only man who did nothing to deserve death, and they were just like us—average. So, before we think we are above this commandment, let's remember that all of us are full of sin and capable of atrocious evils.

Reflection Questions

1. Have you ever thought this commandment was kind of obvious? Why?

2. How do you feel knowing your own heart is sinful enough to act in this way?

Prayer

Father, we know our hearts are sinful before you. We ask that you help us to walk away from our sin and deeper into the love of Christ. Keep us from anger, vengefulness, and division that could cause us to sin against you. Forgive us when we have been unrighteous in our anger. Amen.

Day 60

Q. What is required of us in the sixth commandment?

A. The sixth commandment requires us to preserve all human life.

Do not be surprised, my brothers and sisters, if the world hates you. We know that we have passed from death to life, because we love each other. Anyone who does not love remains in death. Anyone who hates a brother or sister is a murderer, and you know that no murderer has eternal life residing in him.

—1 JOHN 3:13–15

HUMAN LIFE IS VALUABLE, not because of anything we bring to the table, but because of God's free decision to give it value. We are not valuable because we do good things or because we have the potential to be great and to change the world. No, we are valuable because God, the Creator and Sustainer of all things, has said so. In Genesis 1:27, we read, "So God created mankind in his own image, in the image of God he created them; male and female he created them." God has created us and given us value by making us like him. We image the living God of the universe.

Therefore, to snuff out one of these lives is strictly forbidden. When we think murder is justifiable or okay, we not only bring harm to another human being, but we also deface the image of God that is present in each person. All human life has value, whether it's young or old, black or white, smart or dumb, unborn or born, sick or healthy. We are not in God's position to take life and deprecate his image in human beings. Full stop.

Unfortunately, no matter what time period you look to in history you will find the senseless killing of people to be commonplace. The track record of human beings upholding the lives of those different than them, upholding the lives of those less fortunate, and upholding the lives of those unborn has been a story of tragic loss. We see, time after time, unjust killings and genocides as we flip through the pages of our history books, with the twentieth century being the bloodiest of all. Thus, we need to be reminded that every person is created in God's image as an act of his free grace and is worthy of life. Therefore, the sixth commandment requires us to preserve all human life.

Reflection Questions

1. What is it about human beings that makes them so valuable and worthy of life?

2. How do you accidentally slip into seeing others as not created in God's image?

Prayer

Thank you, Lord, for creating us in your image. Thank you that every human being has value and worth as your creation. We pray that we might look to you for our salvation. Help us, Lord, to love people as being created in your image. Amen.

DAY 61

Q. What is forbidden in the sixth commandment?

A. The sixth commandment forbids the ending of all human life.

And for your lifeblood I will surely demand an accounting. I will demand an accounting from every animal. And from each human being, too, I will demand an accounting for the life of another human being. "Whoever sheds human blood, by humans shall their blood be shed; for in the image of God has God made mankind. As for you, be fruitful and increase in number; multiply on the earth and increase upon it."

—GENESIS 9:5–7

WHILE NOT MURDERING MAY seem obvious to us, the idea that all people are valuable as beings created in God's image is not. The sad reality is that many people have spread ideas that fundamentally challenge the notion that people are created in the image of God. Usually, the way this plays out is by someone—or a group of people—saying that another group of people are sub- or less than human.

This is what happened in Nazi Germany, which allowed them to ruthlessly exterminate 6 million Jews. Germany adopted an ideology which gave people differing values based on their abilities. Rather than see people as valuable because of something bestowed upon them, they saw people as valuable based on what they brought to the table. This meant that the bestowal of human value was stripped from the hands of God and given to sinful men who, unsurprisingly, created a system of value which interpreted ability through the lens of race and strength. This ideology allowed for unprecedented death and destruction. Aleksandr Solzhenitsyn, in his monumental *The Gulag Archipelago,* writes, "Thanks to ideology, the twentieth century was fated to experience evildoing on a scale calculated in the millions. This cannot be denied, nor passed over, nor suppressed."*

The horrific truth that some people don't see others as valuable is even true in our day. Some people choose to believe that the world began to exist independent of a Creator and that all life evolved by random chance. For them, human beings are merely a product of chance evolution and are no more valuable than any other creature. They essentially believe we are large sacks of meat in which biochemical reactions create thoughts and feelings. Therefore, like in Nazi Germany, the idea that all people are valuable becomes meaningless. In fact, in some cases it may be beneficial to kill off some of the weaker people in order to ensure that only the strongest continue the human race forward. This notion is preposterous and extremely dangerous. If humans are not considered valuable from some outside source, then we have no reason to avoid murdering, killing, and destroying. We can simply create a system that allows these things to take place. Rather, if we want to see people as valuable, we must see them as created in God's image, worthy of protection and dignity no matter the circumstance of their lives.

Reflection Questions

1. What made Nazi ideas so dangerous and how do we do the same thing?

2. How can we work to see all people as created in God's image and, therefore, valuable?

Prayer

Father, we pray that we might look to you alone as the God of the universe. Show us more of your Son Jesus Christ, and fill us with your Holy Spirit. Lord, forgive us where we have failed to see your image in a fellow human being. Help us to treat everyone with respect, dignity, and love. Amen.

*Solzhenitsyn, *Gulag Archipelago,* 78.

DAY 62

Q. What is the seventh commandment?

A. The seventh commandment is to not have sex outside of marriage.

You shall not commit adultery.

—EXODUS 20:14

THIS COMMANDMENT IS POTENTIALLY the most difficult to discuss given the current cultural climate. As a society we worship at the feet of sexuality. We are constantly seeking sexual encounters to fulfill our lustful desires. In fact, nowadays, sexuality is even used as a way to describe our primary identity as human beings. We describe ourselves in relation to our sexual proclivities using terminology like "heterosexual," "gay," "straight," "lesbian," "bisexual," and many other identity markers which can be summed up in an ever-growing acronym. We live in a world with websites, apps, and other things which are designed to prevent us from being obedient to God's word about sex.

Here we must acknowledge that this commandment has sometimes been used unjustly. At times it has been used as a bludgeon to mark someone as impure and unfit for the kingdom of God. There is certainly truth in the claims of some who push back against the Christian teaching on sexuality that failure to obey has been deemed a super-sin. Certainly there is truth in the claim that some treat disobedience in this area so seriously that it effectively makes someone irredeemable. While it is self-evidently true that the Scriptures teach us that sex outside of the holy union of marriage as defined by the Bible is wrong, this does not mean that those who have broken this commandment are irrevocably lost. Rather, "If you declare with your mouth, 'Jesus is Lord,' and believe in your heart that God raised him from the dead, you will be saved" (Rom 10:9). Our belief in Christ is what saves us from our sins, and it is through belief in him that we are able to repent and walk away from our sinfulness.

Even so, this commandment remains important in our daily lives and, therefore, we should live into its teaching. While the cultural cry is one that screams sexual liberation and freedom, we as Christians push back because we cannot accept this as a path to human flourishing. We know that the absence of shame is not freedom but complete enslavement to the power of sin. Only faithfulness to the God of the Bible leads to the flourishing of humanity, and for that reason we must take seriously the commandments he has given us.

Reflection Questions

1. Have you ever felt like sexual sin is a *super-sin,* and how does the gospel deny this?

2. Why is it important that we continue to take this commandment seriously?

Prayer

Heavenly Father, we long to honor you not only with our words but also with our bodies. Lord, help us to keep ourselves holy in the area of sexual fidelity. Forgive us where we have failed in this area through your Son Jesus. Amen.

DAY 63

Q. What is required of us in the seventh commandment?

A. The seventh commandment requires us to protect our purity and the purity of others.

Flee from sexual immorality. All other sins a person commits are outside the body, but whoever sins sexually, sins against their own body. Do you not know that your bodies are temples of the Holy Spirit, who is in you, whom you have received from God? You are not your own; you were bought at a price. Therefore honor God with your bodies.

—1 CORINTHIANS 6:18-20

"SEX SELLS," SAYS THE old adage. Sadly, it is not wrong. We see sexual content everywhere we look precisely because it sells. We see sex in our TV shows, we see sexual content on Instagram, we see YouTube creators pushing the limits of what is allowed in order to get views, and we even see debates around sexuality on the news. This is the water in which we swim on a daily basis; a deluge of sexualized content meant to draw us in and steal our attention. Yet, those of us who are adopted into the family of God through faith need to be cautious that we are not allowing this environment to shape us in destructive ways.

Instead, our worldview should be shaped by Scripture as we trust in the Holy Spirit to make God's word known to us. Scripture teaches us to practice two things when it comes to our sexuality. First, if we are not married—as defined by Scripture—then we must practice abstinence. Meaning that we must not engage in sexual conduct and we must do all that we can to help others do the same. Second, if we are married then we must be sexually faithful to our spouse. That means we must protect the marriage bed from any possible defilement. Both from without, that is by committing adultery with other people; and from within, that is by falling into lustful fantasies which lead us away from our spouse.

These two things can be hard to accomplish in a culture that is over-stimulated with sexual inputs, but nonetheless it is required of us. The temptations we face are not unbeatable, even in our world. First Corinthians 10:13 says, "No temptation has overtaken you except what is common to mankind. And God is faithful; he will not let you be tempted beyond what you can bear." Even in the midst of our temptations to sin we can be assured that we can overcome them through the power of the Holy Spirit working in us.

Reflection Questions

1. How can you protect yourself from indulging in sexual content?

2. What two practices does the Scripture outline for Christians wishing to serve God faithfully in their sexuality?

Prayer

Holy Father, you designed sex for our good, but like all good gifts we twisted it and distorted it to meet our sinful desires. Help us, Lord, to see sex in light of what your word says about it. Forgive us where we have been shaped by the cultural understanding of sex. Remind us of your love and grace for us in Jesus, we pray. Amen.

DAY 64

Q. What is forbidden in the seventh commandment?

A. The seventh commandment forbids us to act or think in a way that would be damaging to another's purity.

It is God's will that you should be sanctified: that you should avoid sexual immorality; that each of you should learn to control your own body in a way that is holy and honorable, not in passionate lust like the pagans, who do not know God.

— 1 THESSALONIANS 4:3–5

THE SEVENTH COMMANDMENT FORBIDS us from any sexual misconduct outside of marriage as defined by the Bible. This is further clarified when we look to the New Testament. Jesus cuts straight to the heart and says, "But I tell you that anyone who looks at a woman lustfully has already committed adultery with her in his heart" (Matt 5:28). Thus, the Scriptures not only forbid the action of sexual misconduct but also the lustful intentions and thoughts of the heart.

An all-too-common practice, particularly in regards to this commandment, is to try and find *grey areas* which Scripture doesn't explicitly address and then allow these practices because no direct prohibition has been allayed against them. However, this is a distortion of God's word and an affront to the gospel. God's law is perfectly just and all-encompassing. There are no shades of grey which allow for particular sexual activities outside of marriage. While this may be hard to accept, it is nonetheless true. God does not give us a moral code full of loopholes that free us from obedience to the law. All sexual activity outside of marriage is forbidden.

Despite the very clear biblical teaching on this we still find ourselves disobeying this command. Our hearts are sinful and fall far short of the goal set out for us in Scripture. While we should strive to protect each other's purity with all our might—in both thought and deed—none of us have done so to perfection. Thus, we must rest on the love and grace displayed in Jesus Christ's death and resurrection. When we put our trust in him there is "no condemnation" (Rom 8:1). We are saved by his grace and made righteous through the gift of his righteousness to us. And it is only through the relationship we have with him that we can obey the commandments set out for us in Scripture. It's as we are found in Christ and as the Holy Spirit indwells us that we can be obedient to God's word.

Reflection Questions

1. How does Jesus address the heart of the seventh commandment?

2. In what ways do you look for *grey areas* or loopholes to justify disobedience to this commandment?

Prayer

Merciful God, Father in heaven, we pray that we might protect the purity of those around us by not participating in the sexual arbitrariness of our day. Help us to do this well and forgive us when our deeds or thoughts fail us. Remind us of the love you have shown in Jesus Christ by the Holy Spirit, and empower us for obedience through him. Amen.

Day 65

Q. What is the eighth commandment?

A. The eighth commandment is to not steal.

You shall not steal.

—EXODUS 20:15

THEFT IS A CRIME that almost everyone agrees is wrong. Anyone who has been on the receiving end of theft recognizes the frustration of having something that is yours stolen. Yet, this commandment goes beyond acts of theft such as stealing someone's wallet. Rather, it extends to theft of any kind. Theft of property, theft of time, theft of resources, and so on, which means that this commandment prohibits the sluggard from wasting away hours on the job which his employer is paying him for. It means that it prohibits the shady business practices which allow you to hold back money from the government, employees, and more. It means that it prohibits the use of another person's ideas without correctly citing them.

All in all, the prohibition on theft extends to more than we commonly think of when we hear the commandment. In fact, as we examine this commandment and meditate upon it, we should recognize that all of us have broken it. Like the other commandments when we reflect upon it, we are struck by the reality that we are law-breakers. Our reflection transforms the commandment into a mirror which reveals our own sinfulness. Yet, where the law reveals our sinfulness Christ's grace abounds. For "through the law comes knowledge of sin" but "the righteousness of God has been manifested apart from the law . . . for all have sinned and fall short of the glory of God, and are justified by his grace as a gift" (Rom 3:20–24 ESV).

Meditate on this law, recognize your own sinfulness, and be pointed to the grace of Jesus Christ.

Reflection Questions

1. In what ways do you break the eighth commandment? In action? In thought?

2. How does this commandment point us to Christ and remind us of God's grace?

Prayer

Holy Father, you have given us the Ten Commandments so that we might know what righteousness looks like, but in our sin, we never live up to this standard. Our hearts constantly fail you and we regularly break these great commandments. Forgive us, Lord. Thanks be to you for Jesus Christ, who perfectly obeyed these laws and gives us his righteousness through his death and resurrection. We pray that in the power of the Holy Spirit, we might walk in newness of life and obedience to your word. Amen.

DAY 66

Q. What is required of us in the eighth commandment?

A. The eighth commandment requires us to treat other people's possessions as we would want our possessions to be treated.

"Will you steal and murder, commit adultery and perjury, burn incense to Baal and follow other gods you have not known, and then come and stand before me in this house, which bears my Name, and say, 'We are safe'—safe to do all these detestable things? Has this house, which bears my Name, become a den of robbers to you? But I have been watching!" declares the Lord.

—JEREMIAH 7:9–11

THE LENS THROUGH WHICH we can examine our hearts regarding this commandment is given in our answer today. As we reflect on how we are to live this commandment out we simply need to ask ourselves how we might feel if the thing we were about to do was done to us. How might we feel if someone withheld pay from us? How might we feel if our ideas and thoughts were attributed to someone else? How might we feel if something we loved or cherished was taken from us? I think we can all agree that it would not feel particularly good.

Yet, our world is so marred by sin that we actively suggest breaking this commandment in public policy debates. Lately, there has been a massive upsurge in discussions surrounding the redistribution of wealth. The idea being that the wealthy in society are now uber-wealthy and the poor are getting poorer. Therefore, governments should work to "redistribute" money from the wealthy to the poor through taxation and social programs. However, this discussion essentially amounts to a disdain for the wealthy, a coveting of their property, and a desire to see the wealthy stripped of everything they own. I am not suggesting that the wealthy should hoard their goods and money for themselves. This is an equally unbiblical idea and a sin, as Jesus makes clear in the parable of the rich fool (Luke 12:16–21). Rather, the wealthy should act with a heart of radical generosity towards all people as God has acted towards us. Yet, even then, generosity cannot be made compulsory. Compulsory generosity—generosity which leads to jail time if you do not comply with it—is theft. And theft, even by a governing authority, is wrong. Simply ask yourself: If it was your possessions, the things you own right now, how would you feel?

When we answer this simple question, we can get an understanding of how we should respond to the temptation of theft. We should be opposed to it in all forms because it goes against God's law and it does not honor our neighbors. In fact, the premise of our answer goes beyond just this commandment and extends to all of God's law. As Jesus says, "So in everything, do to others what you would have them do to you, for this sums up the Law and the Prophets" (Matt 7:12). We are to treat other people as we would like to be treated by them. This can only be accomplished as we trust in the work of the Holy Spirit who makes it possible for us to love our neighbors.

Reflection Questions

1. What is theft and how does theft harm our neighbors?
2. Jesus outlines the golden rule in Matthew 7:12. How does this apply to theft?

Prayer

Father in heaven, you have given us the things of our life as gifts. Let us hold them loosely and not get tied down by the material things of this world. Forgive us when we steal, cheat, and lie. Empower us by the Holy Spirit to walk away from these sinful tendencies. Amen.

Day 67

Q. What is forbidden in the eighth commandment?

A. The eighth commandment forbids us from taking anything which we do not rightfully own.

"Ever since the time of your ancestors you have turned away from my decrees and have not kept them. Return to me, and I will return to you," *says the Lord Almighty. "But you ask, 'How are we to return?' Will a mere mortal rob God? Yet you rob me. But you ask, 'How are we robbing you?' In tithes and offerings. You are under a curse—your whole nation—because you are robbing me."*

—MALACHI 3:7–9

OUR ANSWER POINTS US toward the concept of rightful ownership. The right to own private property has been a standout feature of most modern Western nations. Yet the question is beginning to arise whether or not private property is actually a good thing. Some people question the idea of private property by arguing that it is merely something which entrenches inequality between classes of people. So, is private property a legitimate biblical concept which we should defend or not? It seems that the answer to this question is both a no and a yes.

The answer is no in the sense that we do not *own* anything that has not been given to us from the Father above. Everything we have is rightfully his as the Creator of all things. He owns all. Yet in his love for us he gifts things to us, from the clothes on our back to the talents we have. Knowing this we should be cautious that we do not attach ourselves too closely to earthly goods. First, they are temporal and will pass away, and secondly, they are God's gifts and therefore an extension of his grace. We don't have a right to them in any sort of *a priori* sense.

On the other hand, we can answer the question above in the affirmative. Yes, we can say we have a right to ownership of certain things if we first see those things as belonging to and being given by God. He has bestowed them on us and entrusted us with them. So, we do have a *right* to private property in the sense that God has given us these gifts and entrusted them to our care. Likewise, our goal with these gifts should be to utilize them for the purposes of furthering God's glory. This means showing love and care for the poor among us through generosity.

The fact that we can answer whether or not we have a right to private property in the affirmative and negative changes our understanding of theft. Theft is not so much about taking something that doesn't belong to you, but it's about taking something that hasn't been given to you. It's fundamentally an attempt to control one's life through unjust means rather than trusting the good giver of all gifts, God Almighty. Theft is forbidden because it takes something that only God has the right to take or give to someone. It's a crime against our neighbor and an affront to God, who has given us good gifts to utilize for his glory. This should lead us to reflect on the truth that all we have is given from above and that with everything we own we are merely stewards for a short period of time. Thus, we should be willing to part with our possessions for the sake of Jesus Christ.

Reflection Questions

1. Do you view your property as a gift from God or rightfully your own?

2. How should you respond to the knowledge that everything you own is a gift from God?

Prayer

Holy, merciful, and loving Father, we pray that we might see all we have and all we are as your gracious gift to us. Lord, we are so prone to make things into idols and to hoard them, as though they are our own. Release our grip on these things so that we might be thankful for them but not attached to them. Show us how everything we are and own is your good gift. Thank you for the gift of your love shown to us in your Son Jesus Christ. Amen.

Day 68

Q. What is the ninth commandment?
A. The ninth commandment is to not lie.

You shall not give false testimony against your neighbor.

—EXODUS 20:16

TIME AND TIME AGAIN we are put into situations where the easiest solution is to tell a white lie in order to avoid the pain and hurt that the truth might cause some other person. Due to this we tend to think that telling a white lie is actually beneficial because, more often than not, it leads to the least amount of hurt and is easier for both parties. Yet, how do we square this thinking with the ninth commandment, which teaches us that it is our obligation to be truthful?

In order to make sense of this we need to go deeper than merely the command itself. Instead, we need to examine the very foundation we use to evaluate something as right or wrong. A good majority of people tend to evaluate whether something is right or wrong by whether it causes pleasure or pain. The objective of a decision is to cause the least amount of pain and therefore the highest amount of pleasure. This moral thinking is called *utilitarianism*. This means that something like telling a white lie is made justifiable because it leads to the least amount of pain.

The problem with this way of thinking is that it presumes that our reason's ability to determine right and wrong is sufficient, it denies the sinful nature of every human being and the effects that has upon our reasoning ability, and it suggests that *moral arithmetic* is a legitimate possibility for judging hard ethical cases. Rather, if we want to be faithful to Scripture then we need to acknowledge that right and wrong have less to do with causing the least amount of pain and more to do with reflecting the image of a perfect God. Right and wrong have more to do with being found in Christ than in our reasoning abilities. Christians believe that this—and only this—will lead to a flourishing human life. Thus, the command forbidding us from lying is good and right because it reflects God's nature: that he is perfectly truthful.

Reflection Questions

1. Have you ever found yourself telling a white lie to protect someone's feelings?

2. Does knowing that God desires us to be truthful as he is truthful change the way you view white lies?

Prayer

Holy Father, give us the strength to be truthful as you are truthful. Teach us what it means to speak the truth in love to one another and protect us from deceit. Help us, Holy Spirit, to run away from lies and towards truth. We pray all this in the name of the Father, Son, and Holy Spirit. Amen.

DAY 69

Q. What is required of us in the ninth commandment?

A. The ninth commandment requires us to speak
the truth about other people.

*You were taught, with regard to your former way of life, to put off your
old self, which is being corrupted by its deceitful desires; to be made new
in the attitude of your minds; and to put on the new self, created to be
like God in true righteousness and holiness. Therefore each of you must
put off falsehood and speak truthfully to your neighbor, for we are all
members of one body.*

—EPHESIANS 4:22–25

IRREPARABLE DAMAGE HAS BEEN done to people's reputations, careers, and
lives because of a lie spoken against them. While this is clearly unjustifiable
and wrong, it seems to take place more and more. Outrage culture and cancel culture have amplified this to the extreme. Likewise, social media has
provided a platform for nefarious predators to disseminate false information with absolutely horrific consequences. People's entire livelihoods have
been ruined by fabricated stories regarding past events, words, or actions
which they purportedly participated in.

Strangely enough, this supposedly modern phenomenon of cancel
culture, is not entirely new. In the book of Genesis, we see something similar happen to Joseph. Joseph is the servant in a wealthy Egyptian household. That is, until the wife of the head of the household lies about him
abusing her and he is thrown in prison. Joseph is given no fair trial, and

there is no examination of evidence; he is simply assumed to be guilty and is summarily locked up (Gen 39). Yet, it is all a lie, put together by a vengeful woman in an attempt to destroy Joseph's life. And while it was a vengeful wife in this story, in our day it could be a vengeful boss, a vengeful ex-lover, a vengeful idealogue, or any number of individuals whose desire to spit invective is more powerful than their desire for a just society.

Now, none of this is to say that people coming forward with stories of abuse shouldn't be taken seriously. Cancel culture sometimes cancels the right people, and where there is crime and evil involved, we see a good example of this. In fact, it should be our wish to see the evil of our society eradicated and prosecuted. However, even this should be done in a measured way, taking into account physical evidence, testimonies, and other means to determine the crimes of the individual. We should not simply take a claim at face value without stopping to see if it is justified. Why? Because false accusations lead to false charges, which produces a false society.

In fact, this is what happened to Jesus. Jesus was not condemned to die because of anything he did, but because false witnesses came forward against him, lied about his ministry, and accused him with trumped up charges (Matt 26:60). And if even the Son of God—perfect in righteousness—can be falsely accused, then certainly accusations can be wrong. What; shall we believe the crowd which shouted "Crucify him?"

Therefore, this commandment requires us to speak truthfully of other people, regardless of how we might feel about them. Even if we feel that they have treated us poorly, broken our hearts, or spurned our affections, we must speak truthfully concerning them. We must watch carefully that we do not use our lying tongues as tools for vengeance. Vengeance is not our work; it is the Lord's (Deut 32:35). We merely leave it to him, trusting that he will judge fairly in the end. Meanwhile we must speak truthfully about others.

Reflection Questions

1. How does lying harm other people, especially lying about others?

2. Have you ever reflected upon the fact that Jesus was crucified based on the testimony of liars?

Prayer

Father, you truly are the God of all truth. Forgive us for the ways in which we have walked in lies. Forgive us for the lies we have told about others. Forgive us for the lies we believe about others. Help us, Lord, to be truthful in all we do. Amen.

Day 70

Q. What is forbidden in the ninth commandment?

A. The ninth commandment forbids us from speaking wrongfully about other people.

There are six things the Lord hates, seven that are detestable to him: haughty eyes, a lying tongue, hands that shed innocent blood, a heart that devises wicked schemes, feet that are quick to rush into evil, a false witness who pours out lies and a person who stirs up conflict in the community.

—PROVERBS 6:16-19

As WE EXPLORED IN the previous section, speaking wrongfully about other people can have dire consequences in their lives. To speak a lie against someone is a serious offense. It's an attempt to destroy them by presenting a false picture of who they are to other people. Just think of all the people throughout history who have been executed as a result of false witnesses, the number is (more than likely) staggering.

God, therefore, reminds his people not to do this precisely because of the implications that go with it. It is extremely easy to present a false image of somebody to someone else, but it is extremely difficult to restore the marred image once it has been defaced. Just imagine the painstaking difficulty of restoring the *Mona Lisa* if someone smeared red paint across her face. It would prove quite challenging. Whether we like it or not, lies have consequences, and unfortunately those consequences are usually felt most deeply by the person we are lying about. This was particularly true when lies led to the most heinous crime the world has ever seen: the death of God incarnate.

Matthew 26:57–68 recounts the story of multiple false witnesses making claims against Jesus, ultimately leading to his sentence of death. This story should remind all of us of the power the tongue holds over a person's life. One word of false testimony can lead a crowd of people to condemn the very Son of God who was perfectly righteous—which is precisely why they would need to lie in the first place. While this is evil in the highest degree, it is also through this death that we are saved. In our sinfulness we break the commandments all the time, but God, through Jesus Christ, made a way for us to be saved. The lies which put him on the cross demonstrated the truth of who he was. These lies were shown to be empty as he continued to act in complete humility, willingly taking his cross to Golgotha, acting in perfect righteousness. The lies were shown to be powerless as he defeated the father of lies on the cross and rose to new life.

Reflection Questions

1. Is it easier to deface an image or to repair one that has been defaced? Do you deface anyone's image?

2. How is it that Jesus defeated the father of lies, and what does this mean for you?

Prayer

Loving Father, thank you for sending your Son Jesus to be the one who took the punishment of sin. Forgive us, Lord, and help us believe in him more. Fill us with your Spirit so that we might see Jesus Christ in new ways. Deepen our relationship with you by showing us your love as a Father, by showing us the love of Jesus, and by empowering us with your Spirit. Amen.

DAY 71

Q. What is the tenth commandment?

**A. The tenth commandment is to not desire
other people's lives or stuff.**

You shall not covet your neighbor's house. You shall not covet your neighbor's wife, or his male or female servant, his ox or donkey, or anything that belongs to your neighbor.

—EXODUS 20:17

IN THIS COMMANDMENT WE are introduced to the term "covet," and from our answer we learn that this means to desire something someone else has. Unfortunately, in our society covetousness is almost built into the fabric of everyday life. As consumers, we are inoculated with a desire for the things other people have and we use our purchasing power to obtain the objects of our covetous lusts.

We see this clearly in advertising. Advertising is all about exploiting our sinful desire for the things we do not own. We see ads of perfect families, or happy couples, or self-motivated single people using some product, insinuating that this particular object will lead to the perfect life. Thus, we buy it at Target the next time we are there. Our covetous desires are so strong that we feel a constant need to "keep up with the Joneses" in our phone purchases, housing choices, clothing styles, and so on. There is a tangible fear of missing out if we don't have the latest greatest thing.

Yet, we don't just covet with respect to what we want to buy or own, but we covet in more extreme ways too. We may desire to take someone else's life out of jealousy or envy, wishing we were more like them. We may desire someone else's spouse and actively attempt to steal them away. However, Scripture clearly teaches us that covetousness, the desire for other people's lives, stuff, spouses, or anything else, is wrong. And it's only when we understand that everything we are, have, and love is a gift from God that the spell of covetousness can be broken.

God was under no obligation to give us life, but out of his grace he did. God was under no obligation to give us the stuff we own, but out of his grace he did. God was under no obligation to put people in our lives that we could love, but out of his grace he did. Everything we have is a gift and if it is all a gift then the fundamental heart attitude we should have towards possessions, livelihoods, and circumstances is thanksgiving. Thanksgiving is the opposite of covetousness. It is the force which deafens covetousness's evil grasp upon our lives. Whereas the covetous see possessions, livelihoods, and circumstances as something they have a right to, the Christian sees these things as gifts from a gracious God who loves them. So, when you notice your heart coveting, reflect upon the gifts of God and lift up prayers of thanksgiving.

Reflection Questions

1. In what ways do you covet, and in what area of life are you most likely to covet?

2. How often are you seeking to thank God for everything in your life?

Prayer

Gracious God, merciful Father, thank you for everything you have given us: homes, cars, phones, health, success, families, and so much more. You are a God who richly blesses us, and we take this for granted every single day. Forgive us, Father, and remind us of the ultimate gift: your Son Jesus, who died for our sins. Let us be content in his love alone by the power of the Holy Spirit. Amen.

Day 72

Q. What is required of us in the tenth commandment?

A. The tenth commandment requires us to be content in the situation God has placed us and with the things he has given us.

But godliness with contentment is great gain. For we brought nothing into the world, and we can take nothing out of it. But if we have food and clothing, we will be content with that.

—1 TIMOTHY 6:6–8

WHEN WE CONSTANTLY DESIRE other people's lives, possessions, and circumstances we inevitably become discontent. Our discontentment grows each day with useless comparisons to other people, using the worlds metrics of success. The problem of discontentment is exacerbated to the umpteenth degree by social media, where the picture of the perfect life is no longer presented to us in advertising form only, but in the lives of the people closest to us.

Everyone has become capable of curating a life *feed* which acts more as an advertisement for oneself than as a real representation of a person's life. Every happy moment, every picture in which we look good, and every success story is shared on social media so that our lives are carefully molded in the eyes of others. In response to this, some people have begun to share their struggles on social media to raise awareness for different causes. However, since it is "chic to be weak," this too is simply another way we curate our lives in order to present an image of ourselves so that others might accept us. We should not be overly cynical here, but perhaps your attempts to raise awareness via social media is only a poorly veiled attempt to raise awareness of you.

The end result of this is the creation of an environment in which people are anxiously seeking after the next best thing, flitting about, and seeking contentment for their weary lives through covetous behavior. The painful discovery, however, is that this pursuit never leads to contentment, but rather more discontentment. Chasing after more money, sex, acclaim, or even just products will never bring the contentment we desire. As popular writer James K.A. Smith said, "we're always on the move, restless, vaguely chasing something rather than oriented to a destination."* Covetousness leads to restlessness, and restlessness leads to thanklessness, which leads to more covetousness, and on and on the cycle goes.

This is why thankfulness is so important. In fact, thankfulness is the key to contentment. If we see all that we own, do, or enjoy as gifts, and come to the throne of God humbly, acknowledging his grace in giving these things to us, then contentment is the end result. It is only when we acknowledge that God has so placed us where we are and given us what we have as a gracious, loving gift that we can learn to practice contentment and stop striving for the next best thing. It is only as we rest in God, acknowledging his grace towards us, that we find rest for our weary souls.

Reflection Questions

1. How are you engaging with social media? Is it in a way that breeds discontentment?

2. What does it mean to rest in God and seek contentment in your relationship with him?

*Smith, *On the Road with Saint Augustine*, 5.

Prayer

Father, we pray that we might not grow discontent with our lives, but would be content with the gifts you have given us. Lord, you have given us so many good things and even if we are poor, materially, you have given us the gift of eternal life with you through Jesus Christ. Forgive us when we spurn these things and chase after toys, money, success, sex, and anything else that shows our discontentment with life. Help us to be thankful for everything you give. Amen.

Day 73

Q. What is forbidden in the tenth commandment?

A. The tenth commandment forbids discontentment with the situation or gifts of God, and forbids a desire to have the same situation or gifts as other people.

I know what it is to be in need, and I know what it is to have plenty. I have learned the secret of being content in any and every situation, whether well fed or hungry, whether living in plenty or in want. I can do all this through him who gives me strength.

—PHILIPPIANS 4:12–13

IT IS NOT ONLY the case that our lives are substantially worse when we are discontent, but it is also that discontentment is forbidden by God. When we are discontent with our lives, we are essentially saying to God that we could do a better job than he is currently doing. We think, in our sinfulness, that if we were God, we would be able to make ourselves content with more money, different talents, other people's affirmation, and so on. We think that if we could just have that thing then our problems would dissolve and our discontentment would be gone.

This is tantamount to saying that God is not capable of the job set before him. That he has somehow messed it all up and that we could do better if we were just given the reins. This brash and enthusiastic arrogance is clearly false. In our sin we have absolutely no idea what would lead to our flourishing. A good example of this can be seen in nature. There is a particular species of fungus which takes over an ant's body, releases chemicals so that the ant leaves the safety of its nest, bids it to climb a nearby tree, and once it has, the fungus releases itself through the ant's head killing the ant in the process. Similar to this zombie fungus, we, in our sin, act under the control of sinful desires which parasitically seek to destroy us and our souls by causing us to act in ways which ultimately lead to our downfall. Thus, even if we were given the reins to control our life, we would do a terrible job. So, what must we do?

We must trust in God. We can't and never will be able to do a better job than God when it comes to our life. He knows all things, he is present at all places, and he is all-powerful. He does what he wills when he wills it, graciously providing for us out of his love. Likewise, God has so willed that we should find our ultimate joy in relationship with him. He has made it so that our freedom is found through resting in him. Therefore, to be discontent in a life where all you have is a gift and where God himself wants to be in a relationship with you is a slap in the face to divine love. Discontentment is sin. It's a refusal to acknowledge God as who he has revealed himself to be—a God of grace, the ultimate giver of all things, the one who wants to see us flourish.

Reflection Questions

1. When you are discontent how do you respond?
2. What gifts has God given you? List out at least ten things.

Prayer

Heavenly Father, help us to be content in you. Let us not chase after the things of this world. Protect us, through the Holy Spirit, from discontentment. Forgive us where we are discontent and let us turn to you for forgiveness. Thank you, Lord, for everything we have and are, but most of all, thank you for Jesus Christ, who took away our sin. Amen.

DAY 74

Q. Is anyone able to perfectly keep the Ten Commandments?

A. No one is able to perfectly keep the Ten Commandments. People continually break them in word, thought, and action.

For all who rely on the works of the law are under a curse, as it is written: "Cursed is everyone who does not continue to do everything written in the Book of the Law." Clearly no one who relies on the law is justified before God, because "the righteous will live by faith." The law is not based on faith; on the contrary, it says, "The person who does these things will live by them."

—GALATIANS 3:10-12

IT SHOULD BE ABUNDANTLY clear by now that no one can claim to have kept all ten commandments perfectly. The law goes beyond simple do-this-don't-do-that language, but gets to the heart of human sinfulness. When Jesus delivered the Sermon on the Mount (Matt 5–7) this is precisely what he revealed, that the law extends to the heart of man and not mere outward appearances.

We see this same idea present in the Gospel of Matthew when a rich young man approaches Jesus, seeking eternal life. This young man asks Jesus what he must do to inherit eternal life, to which Jesus responds, "Keep the commandments" (Matt 19:17). The young man—quick to justify himself—says, "All these I have kept . . . what do I still lack?" (Matt 19:20). It's important to note here that the text gives us no reason to believe that he hadn't kept the commandments outwardly; he isn't lying, but he is misunderstanding the law. Thus, Jesus cuts to the heart of the issue and points out where this rich young man has been disobedient within: "If you want to be perfect, go, sell your possessions and give to the poor, and you will have treasure in heaven" (Matt 19:21). Unfortunately, "When the young man heard this, he went away sad, because he had great wealth" (Matt 19:22). The young man's covetous heart was revealed, his idolatry was exposed, and his unwillingness to serve God alone was made known. His heart was disobedient to the law.

Therefore, even if outwardly we are good people, inwardly we are all law-breakers and deserve the punishment that goes with law-breaking. Psalm 14:3 says, "They have all turned aside; together they have become corrupt; there is none who does good, not even one" (ESV). Likewise, Romans 3:23 says "All have sinned and fall short of the glory of God." We sin in what we say. We sin in how we think about God, ourselves, and others. We sin in our minds every single day. Thus, when we stop and take a hard look at ourselves and reflect on our own goodness, we should recognize that we fall short on every account. Our hope can never be in our own works but rather we must place our hope in God's grace.

And when we come to Scripture this is the very God we see. When God reveals himself to Moses, he says, "The Lord, the Lord, the compassionate and gracious God, slow to anger, abounding in love and faithfulness" (Exod 34:6). God is a God of grace and love towards his people. We see this God revealed to us in the patriarchs, as he cares for Abraham, Isaac, and Jacob, leading them and guiding them in his loving-kindness. We see this God revealed to us in the prophets, where God is concerned for the well-being of his people in gracious love, desiring that the oppressed might be set free. And finally, we see this God revealed to us in the person of Jesus Christ, who willingly went to the cross so that we might be made righteous before God. Therefore, let us not boast of our work, full of sin and disgrace, but let us boast in the work of Christ, who has graciously given us his righteousness.

Reflection Questions

1. What does it mean that obedience to the commandments extends to the heart?

2. Do you view yourself as a law-breaker in need of God's grace?

Prayer

Father, we are horrible sinners constantly in need of your gracious love. Forgive us for our evil thoughts, for the words we have spoken which tear down rather than build up, and for the actions we commit which clearly contradict your word. Help us by the Holy Spirit to rest assured in the grace shown us in Jesus Christ on the cross. Let us put our trust in Christ alone, who gives us his righteousness. Amen.

DAY 75

Q. What does every sin deserve?

A. Every sin deserves God's wrath and judgment.

Then he will say to those on his left, "Depart from me, you who are cursed, into the eternal fire prepared for the devil and his angels. For I was hungry and you gave me nothing to eat, I was thirsty and you gave me nothing to drink, I was a stranger and you did not invite me in, I needed clothes and you did not clothe me, I was sick and in prison and you did not look after me."

—MATTHEW 25:41-43

THE SERIOUSNESS OF SIN demands a response from God. He cannot simply allow egregious sins against his perfect will to go completely unnoticed. Every action has an equal and opposite reaction. In this case the reaction comes in the form of punishment. When we break the law of God, we are liable to the punishment of God. Thus, those who continue to break God's law, who reject Christ as the one who makes them righteous, and who spurn God with their sin, deserve the judgment of God.

However, this judgment is not like any earthly punishment we might face. Because God is of infinite glory, and because every sin is—in one way or another—an action directly committed against this glorious God, the punishment for our crimes must be of equal value. For this reason, Scripture speaks of an eternal judgment for sinners. In Revelation 20:15, we read, "Anyone whose name was not found written in the book of life was thrown into the lake of fire." Likewise, in Matthew 25:41, we read, "Then he will say to those on his left, 'Depart from me, you who are cursed, into the eternal fire prepared for the devil and his angels.'" What awaits the unrepentant sinner is hell.

This is not to suggest that what awaits all those who do not wholly trust in God's grace revealed in Jesus Christ is literal fire. However, it does suggest that there is a real punishment that awaits all who refuse to turn from their wicked ways and trust in God's love revealed in Jesus. The images of hell propagated by Hollywood studios are not an accurate depiction of what Scripture says regarding this judgment. In fact, Scripture has little to say about what hell will actually be like. We are left with the knowledge that it will be bad and that is about it.

Personally, I think the way Michael Bird describes hell does justice to a God of love and of judgment. He writes,

> Hell is the place for creatures who have rejected God's revelation of himself in both nature and in the gospel, who refuse to bow the knee to the one true Lord, and who would rather live in darkness than in the light that exposes them as wicked. I surmise, following N.T. Wright, that persons who have entered into a posthuman state become what they worship—greed, lust, power—and cease to reflect the divine image in any meaningful sense. They arrive at a state beyond hope and beyond pity. Hell, then, is the eternal and punitive quarantining of a humanity that has ceased to be human.*

I am not trying here to diminish the punitive element of hell, but am simply attempting to make sense of this difficult doctrine. Likewise, even this—the loss of all humanity to the lusts of the flesh—would be a punishment almost too burdensome to bear.

When we look to Scripture, we are told that there will be a great judgment of sinners and that this judgment will be everlasting. This is the destiny of all those who sin, including you and me. However, thanks be to God for the work of his Son, Jesus Christ, who made a way for us to be redeemed and brought into eternal life. It's as we believe in him and trust in his love that we are freed from the punishment of hell.

*Bird, *What Christians Ought to Believe*, 217.

Reflection Questions

1. How you do think about hell? Is it a disturbing reality, or a motivating force to trust in Christ?

2. Why is it that sin against God deserves a punishment of such magnitude?

Prayer

Holy Father, we know that all sin deserves eternal punishment. We also know that we are completely undeserving of the love you have shown us in Jesus Christ. Help us, Lord, to see the weight of our sin and the glorious grace of the cross at the same time. We trust, by the Holy Spirit, that Christ has forgiven our sins based upon our confession of faith in him. Amen.

DAY 76

Q. What does God want us to do to be saved from his judgment?

A. God wants us to put our faith in Jesus, to repent from sin, and to accept the benefits that come from Jesus' death.

He then brought them out and asked, "Sirs, what must I do to be saved?" They replied, "Believe in the Lord Jesus, and you will be saved—you and your household." Then they spoke the word of the Lord to him and to all the others in his house.

—ACTS 16:30–32

WHILE WE ARE ALL law-breakers who constantly fail to keep the Ten Commandments, while we all deserve eternal punishment as a result of our gross sins, we are also saved thanks to the grace of God. God, from eternity past, planned to send his Son Jesus Christ at the appointed time to die for our sins. God the Son came as a man, through the Virgin Mary, and perfectly kept the law for our sakes. He experienced the temptations of sin, sympathizing with our weaknesses, yet never sinned (Heb 4:15). Of all the people to ever live he was the only one who didn't deserve God's wrath.

Even so, he took God's wrath for sin upon himself by going to the cross and died a sinner's death. And through this death he defeated the power of sin. He became a propitiation for our sins, offering himself up as a holy and perfect sacrifice. As he was the sacrificial lamb of God, his blood, which poured from his side, wiped the ledger of sin clean for all those who believe in him. He defeated the last enemy, death, by overcoming it through his resurrection, deadening its power. Finally, he ascended to the right hand of the Father where he now rules and reigns over all things.

All of this was accomplished so that whoever repents of sin and believes in the name of Jesus receives God's grace, is justified from their sins, being made right with God, and is sanctified by the Holy Spirit so that they may live a new life of obedience to God's will. This is the gospel message that we proclaim to a dying world: that God entered into this dying world for its sake and died so that the world might live. "For God so loved the world that he gave his one and only Son, that whoever believes in him shall not perish but have eternal life" (John 3:16). It's this message that we trust in for our salvation.

Reflection Questions

1. How did God love the world as it was dying in sin?

2. Do you believe that Jesus accomplished these things on your behalf?

Prayer

Merciful God, Holy Father, help us to see your Son Jesus as our only Savior. Nothing in this world can give us rest besides him— not money, success, relationships, self-identity, nothing. We fully rest on his love through the power of the Holy Spirit. Forgive us when we look to other things for the rest only you provide. Amen.

DAY 77

Q. What is faith in Jesus Christ?

A. Faith in Jesus Christ is receiving and resting in him alone for salvation.

But because of his great love for us, God, who is rich in mercy, made us alive with Christ even when we were dead in transgressions—it is by grace you have been saved ... For it is by grace you have been saved, through faith—and this is not from yourselves, it is the gift of God.

—EPHESIANS 2:4-5,8

WHAT DOES IT MEAN to have faith in Jesus Christ? Often times it seems that what people mean when they say they believe in Jesus is that they think Jesus was a great guy who loved a lot of people and did a lot of good things, but that's about it. They see Jesus as a great teacher, or a guru, but fail to see the Jesus presented in the Bible. They don't see Jesus as God in human flesh, the incarnate deity. They don't see Jesus as the Lord of the universe. They don't see Jesus as a vicarious atonement for sin. Thus, they strip Jesus of his power, his glory, and the honor due his name by making him nothing more than a great man.

However, this understanding of Jesus is completely inadequate if we want to take the Bible seriously. Paul the apostle says that Jesus was "the image of the invisible God" (Col 1:15). In Acts 4:12, we read that "there is no other name under heaven given among men by which we must be saved" (ESV). Likewise, in the prologue to John's Gospel we read that Jesus was the Word become flesh. That he was "in the beginning" with God (John

1:1). In other words, Jesus is not merely some good guy, but the Creator in human flesh.

In theology we would say that Jesus was fully man and fully God. We call this the hypostatic union. Jesus is 100 percent God and 100 percent man. This formulation was worked out in the early days of the church as different sects sought to challenge the doctrine of Christ's divinity. Some believed that Jesus had a physical human body but that his mind or soul was replaced by the divine (Apollinarianism). Some believed that Jesus' humanity was absorbed into the divine nature (Monophysitism). Some divided Jesus Christ into two persons—one the divine person and the other the human (Nestorianism). All of these views were rejected by the early church in favor of the above formulation simply because the above formulation is scripturally based and is the only view which makes sense of the atonement.

To believe in Jesus then, to have faith in him, is to see him as Creator, Sustainer, and Lord of the universe while fully man. It's to rest upon him alone as the God-man who won our salvation. We don't simply emulate the life of Jesus and try to live like him. Rather we firmly believe that he is who he says he is; namely, God. It's because of this that we believe salvation comes from him alone. "Salvation belongs to the Lord" and thus we rest upon the Lord Jesus Christ for our salvation (Ps 3:8 ESV). To believe this is to have faith in Jesus Christ.

Reflection Questions

1. Why do you think it's so important that Jesus is fully God and fully man?

2. How do we have faith in Jesus Christ as our Lord and Savior?

Prayer

Father, thank you so much for the love you have shown us in Jesus Christ. Lord, we wholeheartedly put our trust in him. He is our Savior, our Lord, our God. Help us, Holy Spirit, to see Jesus as our salvation. Forgive us for looking to other things for salvation. Let us trust more in Jesus Christ each day. Amen.

DAY 78

Q. What does it mean to repent of sin?

A. Repentance is when a sinner recognizes his sin, grieves, understands the mercy of God in Jesus Christ, and turns from it towards God.

Have mercy on me, O God, according to your unfailing love; according to your great compassion blot out my transgressions. Wash away all my iniquity and cleanse me from my sin.

—PSALM 51:1-2

SOMETHING WE NEED TO recognize is that repentance is more than simply apologizing. Apologizing easily becomes something we do out of rote memory rather than something we do with humility and honesty. We are taught from a very early age to say "sorry" whenever we do something wrong, such as hit our siblings. This is wise parenting, but it can be quite easy to take this unemotional approach towards apologies into our relationship with God. Thus, we need to recover an understanding of true repentance.

Repentance is not the act of saying sorry, but the act of deep inward conviction of sin and a desire to never commit that act again. It is grief-filled rather than emotionless. In other words, it is not us coming to God and merely saying "I'm sorry," as if this were some magical phrase that he was bound by. God is bound by nothing. Instead, repentance in the Bible is demonstrated in Psalm 51 by King David, where he, convicted of sin, brings it before God, and desires to walk away from evil completely. It's a broken spirit and broken heart before God over our sin.

Therefore, repentance is the precursor to acceptance of the salvation that comes by Jesus Christ. In repentance we turn away from our sin, recognizing it as the disgusting mass it is, and turn toward Jesus Christ as our Savior. In repentance we have our hearts broken by our sin and cast ourselves upon Jesus Christ for salvation. In repentance we weep for our sin, through the work of the Holy Spirit's convicting grace, and seek refuge upon the breast of our wondrous Savior. Often when someone says sorry out of obligation they quickly slip into the same behaviors, but repentance is a complete change of heart where obedience to God's word becomes something desirable. It is not only a turning from sin, but a transformation of our affections. So, repent of your sin and examine your heart. Cast yourself on Christ and he will forgive you.

Reflection Questions

1. How do you approach God—in repentance, or with an apology devoid of all feeling?

2. Where might you need to repent in your life?

Prayer

Heavenly Father, show us the areas of our lives where we need to repent. Convict us of our sins by your Spirit and break our hearts over sin, like you broke David's heart. Remind us of the love of Jesus Christ as we repent. Let us cast all our burdens and sins onto him and trust him for forgiveness. Do this through the power of your Spirit, we pray. Amen.

DAY 79

Q. What can be used to help us grow in our faith in Jesus?

A. What helps us grow in faith in Jesus Christ are his words, the sacraments, and prayer.

For the word of God is alive and active. Sharper than any double-edged sword, it penetrates even to dividing soul and spirit, joints and marrow; it judges the thoughts and attitudes of the heart. Nothing in all creation is hidden from God's sight. Everything is uncovered and laid bare before the eyes of him to whom we must give account.

—HEBREWS 4:12-13

GOD DOES NOT ABANDON us to grow in our faith alone. Just as he doesn't abandon his creation but continually sustains it through his providential care, so he does not abandon us after we've been saved. Aside from his Holy Spirit dwelling in all those who believe, he provides means by which we can grow in our trust of Jesus Christ. God provides us with his words as we find them in Scripture, he gives us the sacraments of baptism and the Lord's Supper, which signify Christ's work on our behalf, and he gives us prayer as a way to come before him and make our needs known to him.

All of these means help us grow in our love for Jesus as we participate in them. God's word found in Scripture reveals his goodness, mercy, and love as he acted in history. He reveals himself to us as we read it and study it. The sacrament of baptism shows us what it means to be buried with Christ in a death like his and raised to new life in a life like his. It symbolizes the washing away of our sin and visibly demonstrates the gospel. The Lord's Supper visibly portrays—through the bread and the wine—Christ's broken body and shed blood for us. Finally, prayer allows us to beseech God with our requests, to praise him, and to offer up thanksgiving for his gifts to us. It is our communication to him, shaped by his communication to us. All of these things are gracious gifts of God so that we may grow in relationship with him and learn to love him completely.

And since God has so graciously blessed us with these means it is imperative that we, with willing obedience, use them in our lives. If you have not been baptized but confess Jesus as Lord, then get baptized. If you do not attend a church which practices the Lord's Supper, then find one that does. If you don't make reading God's word a priority, find time to do so and read it. If you do not spend time in quiet prayer, reflecting on God's goodness as it is shown in Scripture, then make time. These means, which God has given us, are gifts to us, and refusing to participate in them guarantees stunted spiritual growth. Do not spurn God's gracious gifts, but use them to grow into his love.

Reflection Questions

1. Do you participate in these means to grow closer to God: baptism, the Lord's Supper, Scripture, and prayer?
2. What is God calling you to do today to grow in using these means?

Prayer

Father, you are the giver of all good gifts and you gave us the greatest gift, your Son Jesus Christ. Lord, thank you for all the ways we can grow closer to you. Thank you for your word in Scripture, the sacraments, and prayer. We pray that we might make full use of these means and grow closer with you forevermore. Help us, Lord, in this endeavor. Amen.

DAY 80

Q. How does the Bible help us grow in faith in Jesus?

A. The Holy Spirit uses the reading and preaching of the Bible to convict us of sin and to grow us in holiness through faith.

Oh, how I love your law! I meditate on it all day long. Your commands are always with me and make me wiser than my enemies. I have more insight than all my teachers, for I meditate on your statutes.

—PSALM 119:97–99

THE BIBLE IS MORE than a novel. It's more than a work of philosophy. It's more than simply a history textbook, giving us dates and times for events long past. Rather, it is God's revealing of himself to humanity throughout time and space. It is his self-revelation to us for our sakes. And because of this, Scripture helps us to grow in our trust of Jesus Christ as Savior and Lord. As we go to it, read it, study it, and pray through it, we see more of God's love towards us. As we put our trust in Jesus Christ and as the Holy Spirit opens up our eyes to see the will and work of God throughout the Scriptures, we mature in our faith.

It is for this reason that the Bible is extremely important in our walk with the Lord. It is one of God's chosen instruments by which we grow in our knowledge of him and enjoy fellowship with him. Since this is true, we should recognize our need for the Bible in our daily lives. Scripture, as Jesus tells us, nourishes us like food and grows us into maturity: "It is written: 'Man shall not live on bread alone, but on every word that comes from the mouth of God'" (Matt 4:4). Thus, we should not take our reading of Scripture lightly, but we should approach it with a happy reverence as we partake of the delectable feast God has ordained to nourish us.

Similarly, we shouldn't ignore the Bible and read it sporadically as if it may be good for advice here and there. Instead, Scripture is supremely valuable because by it the Holy Spirit works to show us the supremely valuable One, God Almighty. Therefore, as Saint Augustine was told by the Holy Spirit, "take up and read," so should we.* Scripture is his testimony and, ultimately, it grows us in our faith for Jesus Christ.

Reflection Questions

1. Do you think of the Bible as a way that you can grow in relationship with God?

2. How often are you reading Scripture and what does your answer tell you about your love for God?

Prayer

Holy Father, you have chosen to reveal yourself to us in Scripture. We have been entrusted with this glorious deposit for our faith and we ask that you might open our hearts to hear what it has to say. Help us to look to Scripture. Holy Spirit, illuminate our hearts to understand it. Forgive us through Jesus Christ for neglecting it. Amen.

*Augustine, *Confessions*, 209.

DAY 81

Q. How can we use the Bible to help us grow in faith?

A. We can use the Bible by reading it carefully,
trusting its words, and practicing what it teaches.

*Fix these words of mine in your hearts and minds; tie them as symbols
on your hands and bind them on your foreheads. Teach them to your
children, talking about them when you sit at home and when you walk
along the road, when you lie down and when you get up. Write them
on the doorframes of your houses and on your gates, so that your days
and the days of your children may be many in the land the Lord swore
to give your ancestors, as many as the days that the heavens are above
the earth.*

—DEUTERONOMY 11:18-21

THE GREATEST THREAT FACING the church in the West today is the rise of
biblical illiteracy. When we read Scripture for ourselves, study it, and pray
through it, it grows us in our faith, which also grows us in Christlikeness. It
helps to shape us and mold us to act and live more like Jesus. If this is what
Scripture does as we read it, then there can be no doubt that the lack of
Christlikeness in the church is the result of biblical illiteracy. We simply do
not read our Bibles enough to have it shape who we are in a significant way.

As a solution we must—not should, but *must*—read Scripture. We
must take up the Reformation call, *ad fontes* (back to the sources). We need
a return to the viewpoint of the word of God as being authoritative in faith
and life. It's only as we read it, trusting the Holy Spirit to work through it,

that we grow in our faith. It's only as we put into practice what we learn that we grow in Christlikeness. Without a commitment to read Scripture, to study it carefully, we are bound to see an ever-growing trend towards heterodox beliefs.

Therefore, let us learn once again to cherish God's holy word. Let us learn to make God's word a staple of the Christian diet in every Christian home. Let us utilize the moments of family time that we have to read it together, parents and children alike. Let it be the first thing we read in the morning and let it be the last thing we read as we go to bed. We are at a crucial crossroads; we either take up the word and read, finding life therein, or we suffer spiritual malnourishment and slowly meet our demise. Take up God's word and find life by the power of the Holy Spirit as you trust in Jesus Christ while you read.

Reflection Questions

1. Would you describe yourself as biblically illiterate?

2. Do you read Scripture carefully, trust it, and practice what it teaches?

Prayer

Gracious and merciful Father, we are so grateful for the Living Word, Jesus Christ, who we see fully revealed in your written word, holy Scripture. Forgive us for our neglect of this wonderful word. Forgive us for the idols we turn to instead of your word. Forgive us for caring more about earthly things, like our phones, than knowing you. Holy Spirit, empower us to read. Give us grace, we pray. Amen.

DAY 82

Q. How do the sacraments help us grow in faith in Jesus?

A. The sacraments help us grow in faith in Jesus
by pointing us to his life, death, and resurrection.

*Remain in me, as I also remain in you. No branch can bear fruit by itself;
it must remain in the vine. Neither can you bear fruit unless you remain
in me. I am the vine; you are the branches. If you remain in me and I in
you, you will bear much fruit; apart from me you can do nothing*

—JOHN 15:4-5

THERE IS A WAR in our day on rituals and rites of passage as being, at best,
superstitious nonsense, and at worst, structures of domineering power. For
some reason, many so-called "thinkers" believe that ritual restricts the reasoning capacity of mankind. Ritual is seen as leading people further into
untruth and away from human progress. This could not be further from the
truth. Every institution or organization has particular symbols and ritualistic rites that are performed to remind them of the things they have come
to believe. Even in our secular culture there are particular rites of passage
which we continue to practice for no apparent reason other than they mark
moments of freedom toward more hedonistic pleasures. A sweet sixteen
party or, in the United States, turning twenty-one, are good examples.

In Christianity, unlike in the secular world, these rites don't point us to
ourselves, but point to something outside of us: Jesus Christ. We call them
sacraments and they have been instituted in accordance with holy Scripture
as visible signs or representations of Christ's life, death, and resurrection.
The sacraments are not magical incantations or ritualistic performances

which can move God's will and bend it to meet our needs. This is not what Christian theology teaches even if it is what its cultured despisers might view them as. Rather, they are symbols of things already accomplished on our behalf.

For this reason, as the sacraments are performed in our churches, we can look to them and be reminded of the work of Christ for us. These rituals visibly demonstrate dying to sin and being raised to new life. They visibly demonstrate Christ's brokenness for us on the cross. They visibly demonstrate the outpouring of his blood that washes away our sin. Thus, as we participate in them and see them as pointers to greater realities already accomplished for us, we grow in our love for Christ and his work on our behalf.

Reflection Questions

1. What are some examples of rituals that our secular culture participates in?

2. How do the sacraments point us to Jesus Christ?

Prayer

Father, thank you for giving us visible signs that point us to the life, death, and resurrection of Jesus Christ. Help us to see your great work through and in them. Show us your Son through your divinely instituted means. Amen.

DAY 83

Q. What are the sacraments of the New Testament?

A. The sacraments are baptism and the Lord's Supper.

Those who accepted his message were baptized, and about three thousand were added to their number that day. They devoted themselves to the apostles' teaching and to fellowship, to the breaking of bread and to prayer. Everyone was filled with awe at the many wonders and signs performed by the apostles.

—ACTS 2:41–43

WHEN WE TURN TO the New Testament, we find two sacraments: baptism and the Lord's Supper. Both of these institutions point us to the death and resurrection of Jesus Christ. Both remind us of his lordship over our lives. Both remind us of the gracious love God showed towards us in his Son, Jesus Christ. These sacraments were instituted by Jesus for the sake of the church as continual reminders of the work he did for us. They are visual representations of Christ's saving work that accompany the preached word.

As modern people we often don't like ritualistic elements incorporated into our religious services. Many of us have been shaped by years of indoctrination regarding superstitious beliefs, so we tend to look down on rituals such as the sacraments as having little value for our lives. We prefer to apply science and reason to our worship of God and we tend to shun things we might think are opposed to this narrative. Yet we are creatures of habit. No matter who we are, no matter what we do in life, we all form ritualistic habits that we perform each and every day.

For example, we might tell ourselves that such-and-such an activity will help our favorite sports team win the game. We might wear a jersey in support of that team for instance. Or if we play a sport, we might have a pregame ritual we perform which ensures our success. Perhaps we tap the bat on our cleat before we go up to hit or tape our hockey stick in a particular pattern. These are just some examples among many that could be cited to show our ritualistic tendencies. It's almost as if ritual is fundamental to the human experience.

Any skepticism we might have toward the sacraments should therefore be questioned. We shouldn't be keen to ignore or remove these things from our worship simply because they aren't tasteful to the modern mind. Rather, when we understand the sacraments correctly, we can give up our modern superstitions and see that they function as pictures. Pictures of the death and resurrection of Christ. They are visible representations of the truth we find in the written word of God.

Reflection Questions

1. What are the two sacraments, and have you ever seen them done in your church?
2. Why are the sacraments important parts of our worship to God?

Prayer

Holy Father, thank you for the visible symbols you have given us to teach us about Jesus Christ. Help us to see the great truths of his death and resurrection demonstrated in baptism and the Lord's Supper. Amen.

Day 84

Q. What is baptism?

A. Baptism is when a believer is immersed in water in the name of the Father, the Son, and the Holy Spirit. It symbolizes our death to sin and being raised to new life with Jesus.

Or don't you know that all of us who were baptized into Christ Jesus were baptized into his death? We were therefore buried with him through baptism into death in order that, just as Christ was raised from the dead through the glory of the Father, we too may live a new life. For if we have been united with him in a death like his, we will certainly also be united with him in a resurrection like his.

—ROMANS 6:3-5

THERE IS A UNIQUE, symbolic quality about water. We find this not only in the Bible but also throughout history and culture. For, "as everyone knows, meditation and water are wedded forever."* Water is the source of life; nothing can survive without it. Water grows our food and cleanses our bodies. It's the first thing scientists look for on other planets. Water is a universal human experience, it is universally significant for all of humanity and all of life on earth.

This fact is also true within Christianity. Jesus Christ is said to provide "living water" (John 4:10). Heaven will have the "river of the water of life" flowing through it (Rev 22:1). When Jesus was murdered upon the cross and he appeared lifeless, the soldiers thrust a spear through his side and out

*Melville, *Moby Dick*, 26.

174

came a deluge of water and blood (John 19:34). Not to mention all the other references to water in Scripture: the waters before creation, the parting of the waters at the Red Sea, the water from the rock, the water of Gideon's fleece, and so much more. There can be no doubt regarding the significance of water throughout the Bible.

Similarly, water is significant in the rite of baptism. Its cleansing power is highlighted as the believer is immersed beneath its surface to demonstrate the washing away of sin through Jesus Christ. The punishment of sin is communicated as the believer is held beneath the water's gleaming edge, showing their death to sin. Christ's life-giving power is demonstrated through baptism as the believer is lifted up from the perilous depths, teaching that death has been defeated.

All of this makes baptism an important sacrament in the life of the church. It's a visible symbol of what takes place in our life when we put our trust in Jesus. We die to sin, are no longer enslaved to its powers, and are made alive in Christ. To put it simply, baptism is a visual representation of what happens within us when our faith is put in Jesus Christ.

Reflection Questions

1. Why is water such an important substance for each and every human being?
2. What does baptism tell us about what happens to someone when they believe in Jesus?

Prayer

Father, thank you for the Living Water, Jesus Christ, who is the Lord of our lives. Thank you for baptism, which points us to the reality that we have died to sin and have been raised up with Christ. Forgive us where we fall into sin as we await the day of our full cleansing. Keep us by your Spirit, we pray. Amen.

DAY 85

Q. Who is baptism for?

A. Baptism is for anyone who publicly professes their faith in Jesus Christ and their obedience to him.

Then Philip began with that very passage of Scripture and told him the good news about Jesus. As they traveled along the road, they came to some water and the eunuch said, "Look, here is water. What can stand in the way of my being baptized?" And he gave orders to stop the chariot. Then both Philip and the eunuch went down into the water and Philip baptized him.

—ACTS 8:35–38

ALL CLUBS, ORGANIZATIONS, AND even relationships have some sort of entrance requirements. This is simply one of those things that is true no matter where you go. Every group has some way of seeing who is *in* and who is out. You can't get married unless you are in love and the other person agrees to your proposal. You can't join a social club without first being admitted via an interview process or application to determine if you fit the mold. Similarly, religious faiths have rites of initiation which mark a person as belonging to that particular community.

In Christianity, the rite of initiation practiced is baptism. In order to participate in baptism someone needs to profess faith in Jesus Christ as Lord and Savior of their life. We must be careful here; baptism is not a belief-producing, magical incantation performed by a mediator to the divine. It does not create belief, but rather it's an affirmation of a believer's preexisting commitment to the Lord Jesus Christ. It is a public declaration of faith in Christ. Baptism comes after conversion, as we see all throughout Scripture.

While no church has openly taught that baptism brings about conversion there can be no doubt that the teaching on baptism has been muddled in the past to suggest that it cleanses those who participate in it of their original sin allowing them to live a holy life after participation regardless of their belief. This teaching must be avoided for two reasons. First, because it is found nowhere in Scripture. Secondly, because it undercuts the doctrine of salvation by grace through faith alone.

What we see in Scripture is Christ commanding his followers to "make disciples of all nations, baptizing them in the name of the Father and of the Son and of the Holy Spirit" (Matt 28:19). Throughout the book of Acts we see baptism performed not before but after people come to believe in Jesus. Therefore, baptism is for anyone of any nationality who professes belief in Jesus as their Lord and Savior.

Before we close this brief section on baptism I would like to return to the idea of *in* groups and *out* groups. I recognize that this statement is controversial, especially in our world. The idea that some people are outside the camp seems retrograde and, simply put, mean. Yet, the fact of the matter is that all of us are bound by particular group requirements no matter who we claim to be. We all belong to some group, some community, which determines whether we are *in* or *out*. This is normal and good. In fact, we need this to function as a society. For the church, baptism is the way we mark someone as *in,* as belonging to, a particular church community.

Reflection Questions

1. How does baptism make you a part of a group of local believers?

2. Why is the idea that there are *in* groups and *out* groups so distasteful in our culture?

Prayer

Holy Father, you are the God of all the universe. The one over, in, and above all things. We don't deserve your gracious love, but you've shown it to us in Jesus Christ. Lord, help us to proclaim Christ as Lord and remember our baptism. Forgive us where we have failed to publicly profess our faith. Give us strength to share the Love of Jesus. Amen.

DAY 86

Q. What is the Lord's Supper?

A. The Lord's Supper is when we eat bread and wine as Jesus did during the Last Supper. It symbolizes that his body was broken for us and that his blood was shed for us on the cross.

While they were eating, Jesus took bread, and when he had given thanks, he broke it and gave it to his disciples, saying, "Take and eat; this is my body." Then he took a cup, and when he had given thanks, he gave it to them, saying, "Drink from it, all of you. This is my blood of the covenant, which is poured out for many for the forgiveness of sins."

—MATTHEW 26:26-29

LET US NOT THINK that we can take the Lord's Supper too seriously. It is a serious affair. Paul writes to us in 1 Corinthians 11:27: "Whoever, therefore, eats the bread or drinks the cup of the Lord in an unworthy manner will be guilty concerning the body and blood of the Lord" (ESV). The Lord's Supper is not something to be trifled with. Unfortunately, we sometimes come to the table with a *laissez-faire* attitude, which does not do justice to the symbolism of what is taking place before our eyes in this glorious meal. It is, as Jesus tells us, a symbol of remembrance for his death.

When the minister breaks the bread, we should be reminded of Christ's broken body for us on the cross. Battered by the guards, whipped till his body split, thorns thrust on his head, black and blue to the point of being unrecognizable. A broken body shown in broken bread. And as the cup of wine is drunk, it symbolizes the blood that streamed forth from his wounds. Wounds from the beatings he received. Wounds from the nails that pierced his hands and feet. Wounds filled with the dust and dirt of his travel to Golgotha. A bloody body shown in a cup of wine.

These elements, the bread and wine, symbolize pain—unimaginable pain. Pain endured on our behalf. Pain endured so that our sins may be forever dealt with through his vicarious atonement. Thus, when we come to the table of the Lord, whether it be each week or sporadically through the year, we should examine ourselves. We should pray and confess our sins. Then, and only then, may we take, eat, and drink as a great reminder of the forgiveness won by Jesus Christ.

Reflection Questions

1. What was your attitude surrounding the Lord's Supper before reading this?

2. How has Jesus suffered on our behalf and do you ever meditate on this suffering?

Prayer

Jesus, you suffered on our behalf. You took the worst punishment imaginable so that we wouldn't have to endure any punishment. You have bought our salvation with your life. May we honor your love for us with love for you. Help us, Holy Spirit, to honor the communion table. Let us examine ourselves and confess our sins. Forgive us for our ignorance. Amen.

DAY 87

Q. What should we do before we take the Lord's Supper?

A. We should seek repentance for our sin and to seek reconciliation with our brothers and sisters in Christ.

So then, whoever eats the bread or drinks the cup of the Lord in an unworthy manner will be guilty of sinning against the body and blood of the Lord. Everyone ought to examine themselves before they eat of the bread and drink from the cup. For those who eat and drink without discerning the body of Christ eat and drink judgment on themselves.

—1 CORINTHIANS 11:27–29

EACH TIME WE PARTICIPATE in the Lord's Supper we are brought back to the foot of the cross to witness—in symbolic form—the event of Golgotha. It is a visible pointer to the wounded and broken Jesus Christ, who endured all this hurt on our behalf so that our sins may be forgiven. To hold onto our sin, to leave it unconfessed, to refuse to seek repentance for the wrong-doings we have committed, is not to come to the cross of Christ in humble submission to his work. Instead, when we do this, we spurn the work of the cross as unnecessary for our life.

Similarly, the cross of Christ is the ultimate reconciler of people. It brings people into the family of God through the Holy Spirit no matter the background. Christ, through his work on the cross, tears down the "dividing wall of hostility," making reconciliation possible for all people (Eph 2:14), whether it be familial reconciliation, racial reconciliation, or any other kind of division. To seek reconciliation in any other way is merely a farce. Even if it appears that a relationship has been restored, true forgiveness has not

181

been accomplished because of the failure to go to the one who offers true forgiveness, Jesus Christ.

This also means that to hold onto arbitrary division, to refuse to forgive our brothers and sisters in Christ, to allow bitterness to prevent our love to extend towards another person, is to spurn the work of the cross. We are, in effect, saying that it is incapable of breaking down every division. Therefore, when we come to the table and participate in the Lord's Supper we need to repent of our sins and reconcile with our brothers and sisters in Christ. If we do not do this, we merely "drink judgment" upon ourselves (1 Cor 11:29).

Reflection Questions

1. When you take the Lord's Supper do you think to confess your sin and seek to make your relationships right with your fellow believers?

2. Why do you think it is so important to repent of sin and to seek reconciliation before participating in the Lord's Supper?

Prayer

Heavenly Father, thank you for the love you have shown us. Thank you, Jesus, for offering yourself up on the cross for our sins. We confess our sin to you. Too often we lie. Too often we cheat. Too often we steal. Too often we break your commands. Yet, you have forgiven us through your death. Help us, Lord, to seek reconciliation with those people who have hurt us or whom we have wronged. Holy Spirit, give us the strength to accomplish this. Amen.

Day 88

Q. What is prayer?

A. Prayer is communication with God where we ask him to fulfill things in agreement with his will, where we confess our sins, and where we praise him for the love he has shown us in Jesus Christ.

I write these things to you who believe in the name of the Son of God so that you may know that you have eternal life. This is the confidence we have in approaching God: that if we ask anything according to his will, he hears us. And if we know that he hears us—whatever we ask—we know that we have what we asked of him.

—1 JOHN 5:13-15

ALL GOOD RELATIONSHIPS ARE predicated upon the act of communication. You cannot claim to be close with a friend if you have not gotten to know them through conversation. A husband cannot claim to be in a healthy relationship with his wife if he treats marriage as a business contract devoid of any meaningful conversation and fellowship. Communication is an essential component in any good relationship. It is the bread and butter of any person-to-person contact.

Likewise, our relationship with God is predicated upon communication. Yet, this communication isn't built upon our initiative, but his. We don't start the conversation, he does. And he has started this conversation with us through what we have received in his written word, the Holy Bible. It's as we interact with God's communication to us that we come to him with praise, thanksgiving, confession, and petitions. God invites us to draw near to him and interact with his words in prayer.

But how could we, sinful man, ever approach God in prayer? How could we, so marred by the stains of sin and death, ever dare to come before a holy God and have a conversation with him? We can't. There is no hope for us as sinners to enter into genuine fellowship with God. It simply is not possible. However, God reconciled himself to us through his Son, Jesus Christ, making fellowship with him possible. It's through the work of God's grace, made manifest in Jesus Christ and revealed to us by the Holy Spirit, that we can begin conversing with the God of the universe.

Since Jesus Christ has reconciled us to God, making us sons and daughters of a holy Father, we come to him and speak with him freely. Because God has set his heart on us, he hears our prayers, and out of his sovereign will for our lives, he answers them. In addition to all this, our inadequacies in prayer don't prevent God from hearing our real needs. The Spirit searches our hearts and brings our needs before God, who knows us perfectly (Rom 8:26). Go to God, thank him, confess your sins to him, and praise him for his great love.

Reflection Questions

1. How does seeing prayer as initiated by God change the way you view it?

2. Would you say your prayers rest in the knowledge that God hears you and loves you?

Prayer

Good Father, hear our prayer. We need you desperately. Show us through your word your love towards us. Let us trust in you alone. Thank you for all your good gifts and we pray that all our needs would be met out of your grace. Holy Spirit speak on our behalf and intercede for us. Amen.

DAY 89

Q. What has God given us to direct our prayers?
A. God has given us the Bible, and in that, the Lord's Prayer.

In the same way, the Spirit helps us in our weakness. We do not know what we ought to pray for, but the Spirit himself intercedes for us through wordless groans. And he who searches our hearts knows the mind of the Spirit, because the Spirit intercedes for God's people in accordance with the will of God. And we know that in all things God works for the good of those who love him, who have been called according to his purpose.

—ROMANS 8:26–28

IT SHOULD BE CLEAR by now just how important the Bible is for the life of the believer. Everything we do as Christians is shaped by what we find in this holy book. As we have seen already, when we go to the Bible, we learn about who God is and what he has done for his people throughout history. The Holy Spirit works in our hearts to make the Scripture meaningful to us while we read it. It is *the* way we grow in our knowledge of God, *the* way we grow in our obedience to God, and *the* way we grow in fellowship with God.

Since Scripture has such a primary place in our lives as followers of Jesus, it, quite naturally, shapes everything we do and how we think about God, including how we pray. If Scripture is God's words to us then we can utilize Scripture as a conversation partner in our dialogue with God Almighty. While this illustration is incomplete think of it as a text message. The words of the text message are not that person speaking directly to you as in a face-to-face conversation. Yet, the content of the text, the written words, are used for conversation. You can read the words in the text and respond with a phone call, a written response, or even face-to-face conversation. Scripture functions in a similar way. It is the content that informs our conversation with God.

A more specific example of this would be the prayer we received from Jesus known as the Lord's Prayer. This short prayer—which we find recorded in Scripture—is Jesus' teaching on how we should pray and what we should pray about. In the coming question-and-answers we will elaborate on this prayer, line-by-line, but for now you should recognize that even this prayer is informed by the wider testimony of Scripture. Jesus is not revealing things about God in this prayer which are not already present in Scripture. Thus, when it comes to our prayer life, the best thing we can do is to pray with an open Bible.

Reflection Questions

1. Why is the Bible important in our prayer life?

2. What are some ways that you can begin to incorporate Scripture reading into your prayer time?

Prayer

Father, you have given us your word which shows us your character, holiness, and mercy. Embolden us to read it, study it, meditate upon it, and to pray from it. Holy Spirit, do this work in our hearts and show us how all of Scripture points to the person and work of Jesus Christ. Amen.

DAY 90

Q. What does the first line of the Lord's Prayer teach us?

A. The first line of the Lord's Prayer teaches us that God is our Father, that we can come to him with our requests, and that he sovereignly rules the universe in heaven.

And when you pray, do not keep on babbling like pagans, for they think they will be heard because of their many words. Do not be like them, for your Father knows what you need before you ask him. This, then, is how you should pray: "Our Father in heaven."

—MATTHEW 6:7–9A

JESUS TEACHES US TO pray by giving us an example called The Lord's Prayer. In this prayer each line teaches us something about how to pray and about the character of God. The first line begins with the refrain "Our Father," immediately pointing us to the relationship we have with the God of the universe through Jesus Christ by the power of the Holy Spirit (Matt 6:9). When we put our trust in Jesus Christ we are adopted into the family of God and God becomes our Father. He fulfills our need for fatherly care, love, correction, and teaching like no earthly father ever could.

This does not mean that God is exactly like an earthly father. This would be terrible if it were true. Many people do not have fathers who showed them love, care, and affection. Perhaps some people have even been abused in horrific ways by their fathers, and thus find this teaching to be an exceptionally hard pill to swallow. If the only image of fatherhood you know is one of abuse and pain, then seeing God as Father can be nearly impossible, but we need this teaching.

We need it for a few very important reasons. First, the language of God as our Father is meant to show us that his promised inheritance of eternal life is now ours. In fact, we have been "sealed with the promised Holy Spirit" as the "guarantee of our inheritance" (Eph 1:13–14 ESV). Secondly, the language of fatherhood shows us that we have been made a part of God's family. We have become his children (Gal 3:26). Thirdly, this is the way God has chosen to reveal himself to us in Scripture. Whatever our situation may have been, whatever our thoughts on our earthly fathers, God has chosen to use the familial relationship of a Father to his children to show us how he relates to us. This is a beautiful reality as God is the perfect Father who never turns his children away.

Furthermore, our Father is located in heaven. This is not to say that he isn't also present with us at each moment of the day, but it's to show his sovereign rule over all things. It is to say that he is the king of the universe. Not only do we have a Father whose love is greater than any earthly father, but he is also the king of the universe. Taking all of this into account we should not be afraid of where life will lead and what will happen to us. Our heavenly Father watches over us in his love, sovereignly controlling the universe and working everything out for our good.

Reflection Questions

1. Do you find it hard to accept God as your Father, or do you find it easy? Why?

2. Why is it important that God is our Father in heaven?

Prayer

Our Father in heaven, you love us beyond our wildest imaginations. You gave your own Son, who willingly went to the cross, just to show your love for us. You deserve all the praise, all the honor, and all the glory we can give. Father, you rule everything in creation for the good of your people. You are in heaven, guiding everything so that we might grow in our relationship with you. Forgive us when we fail to see this and fail at our responsibilities to follow you. Amen.

DAY 91

Q. What do we pray for in the second line of the Lord's Prayer?

A. In the second line of the Lord's Prayer we pray that God may be praised above all else by all creatures.

Hallowed be your name.

—MATTHEW 6:9B

WHEN WE COME TO trust in Jesus Christ, and as we grow in our relationship with God, learning about who he is, our desire should be to see others share in the love he offers. It's not necessarily that we want them to experience the good things God offers—even though this may be a motivating factor in sharing the gospel—but it's that we want God to be glorified in everything and by everyone. We want to see people honor and worship God because of who he is, not what he offers.

This is what we pray in the second line of the Lord's Prayer: "hallowed be your name" (Matt 6:9b). This line shows us that, above all else, our desire should be to see God praised in all of creation. Sadly, this is evidently not true of today's world. When we look around us, we see a world that walks further and further away from God, not a world that glorifies his name. We see people who are disobedient to his commands and who rage against God at every opportunity. While this is a sad reality of the world, we can be encouraged knowing that all people will bow before God one day.

If this is true, then the implications for our prayer life from this line of the Lord's Prayer are huge. First, it means that we should constantly be praying for all people—neighbors, the leaders of our nations, and even our enemies. We should be praying that the Holy Spirit softens their hearts to the good news of the gospel so that they come to believe in Jesus Christ. Secondly, since this line of the prayer is a declaration of something that will be accomplished, we can rest assured in our prayers that God will be faithful to his word. It's not as if his name won't be hallowed. It will be hallowed, God will be praised, he will be given glory (meaning he will defeat evil), he will bring peace, and he will restore all things. This is the day we long for.

Reflection Questions

1. When you look at your life, do you desire to see God glorified in everything?

2. Why do we need to ask God for his name to be "hallowed?"

Prayer

Holy Father, we ask that your name might be glorified in all creation. We long for the day when every knee will bow before your Son, Jesus Christ. Holy Spirit, we pray that you would move in the lives of people and bring them to a place where they praise your name. Let all things praise you. Amen.

DAY 92

Q. What do we pray for in the third line of the Lord's Prayer?

A. In the third line of the Lord's Prayer we pray that Jesus might return and make all things new.

Your kingdom come.

—MATTHEW 6:10A

WHENEVER WE SPEAK OF Jesus' return, we are talking about an area of theology known as eschatology. This simply means the study of the end times. All Christians should long for the end times as they mark Christ's return and our glorification. Unfortunately, this isn't the case for most of us. Movies and TV shows often portray the end times as a horrific, terrifying event. Therefore, a lot of people are afraid of the end times. It's fire, brimstone, earthquakes, and all sorts of horrors. Yet, when we think about these last days, when we think about Jesus Christ's return, we should be ecstatic with joy.

As followers of Jesus, the end times do not mean hellfire and brimstone, but the beginning of a glorious renewal. It means our taking on resurrection bodies which are no longer susceptible to the pains of this world. It means the perfection of our relationship with God and our ability to see him "face to face" (1 Cor 13:12). It's for these reasons that our prayer for God's kingdom to come should be filled with a sense of urgency and eagerness. We should desire the end, and desire Christ's return. It will be a beautiful and amazing day when God will dwell with his people and "wipe away every tear from their eyes" (Rev 21:4).

Day 92

Each time we pray "your kingdom come" we are prayerfully longing for the day when everything will be perfected. It is an eschatological prayer, full of desire, for something not of this world to enter into this world for the sake of the world. This small phrase encapsulates our desire for new life, our desire for vindication as God's people, and our desire for justice to be dealt to every evil person and institution. Let us long for this day with hopeful desire.

Reflection Questions

1. What is the first thing which comes to mind when you think of the end times?

2. How can you begin to pray with an eager desire for Christ's return?

Prayer

Lord Jesus, we eagerly await your return. Come, Lord Jesus, we pray. We long for the world to be made right. We long for peace and justice. We long to see you face to face. Bring your kingdom, Lord, and empower us, Holy Spirit, to share the joy of Jesus' return with everyone around us. Amen.

DAY 93

Q. What do we pray for in the fourth and fifth lines
of the Lord's Prayer?

A. In the fourth and fifth lines of the Lord's Prayer we pray
that we would be able to submit to God's will in all things.

Your will be done, on earth as it is in heaven.

—MATTHEW 6:10B

WHILE WE PRAY IN eager anticipation for Jesus Christ's return—where he
will restore everything to perfection—we also pray in humble submission
with the knowledge that God is in control and will do everything for our
good in his own time. This line of the Lord's Prayer is a reminder to us of
God's sovereign rule, his providence, his wisdom in all things. This includes
his return to make all things right.

In the previous line of the Lord's Prayer, we were introduced to the
area of eschatology, the return of Jesus Christ. This line is a damper on any
attempts to make that happen through our own means. It is God's will, not
ours, which ushers in the kingdom. Thus, it is a reminder to us that we are
not "to know the times or dates the Father has set by his own authority"
regarding Jesus Christ's return (Acts 1:7). Instead, we humbly submit to
the lordship of the Father, trusting that his will regarding all things is good.

At the same time, this line expresses our desire to see the world ordered according to God's standard. It is a recognition that things are currently not right with the world. There is sin in our own lives, sin in the lives
of others, and—as a result of sin—terrible suffering all around us. Asking
that God's will be done on earth expresses our desire to see the renewal of

all things, morally and physically. It is a longing for the day when sin will be no more and the king of peace will reign.

As we say "your will be done, on earth as it is in heaven" in our prayers, we should be reminded that God is over all things, he is in control, and that his purposes will be accomplished (Matt 6:10b). Likewise, it should encourage us to walk in step with his ways, as they are set out for us in the Bible, while we work to live like Jesus.

Reflection Questions

1. Do you have a genuine desire to see God's will accomplished in the world?

2. How should this line change the way we live our lives?

Prayer

Heavenly Father, may your will be accomplished here on earth. We know that you sovereignly sustain and rule over all things. We want to see people's lives transformed in accordance with your will. We long to see people walk according to your will. Help us, Lord, to be a light in how we love those around us. Amen.

Day 94

Q. What do we pray for in the sixth line of the Lord's Prayer?

A. In the sixth line of the Lord's Prayer we pray that God would provide for us.

Give us today our daily bread.

—MATTHEW 6:11

THE HUMAN CAPACITY TO worry is seemingly infinite. While most of us in the West don't worry about what we will eat that day—or even the next day for that matter—we do worry about other things. We worry much beyond our need to worry. We have traded our worry about basic necessities for worries about ambition, money, emotional well-being, and so on.

In our pursuit of comfort, we anxiously strive for end-goals that have been advertised to us by our peers to the point that we worry we'll never achieve those ends. We worry we about things like our ability to travel the world. We worry about missed experiences and have created an acronym to describe this worry: *FOMO* (fear of missing out). We worry about job opportunities, not because we won't find a job, but becauae we worry the job we find won't be fulfilling. Our worry, in the West, is produced more by peer pressure, advertising, and comfort than it is by need.

The prescribed medicine for this ailment of pseudo-worry comes in the sixth line of the Lord's Prayer. Here we learn two things. First, we learn that our needs are much more limited than we think. Christ calls us to ask for our daily bread. The bare minimum essentials to sustain our lives. This isn't to say that the Lord desires us to be all impoverished, with only a meager portion of bread to sustain us, but rather to show us that our needs are much smaller than we might like to think. Secondly, we learn the Lord will provide for those needs. Christ tells us to "not worry" about food, drink, clothing, and so on (Matt 6:25). He will provide us with these things in his sustaining love and providence over our lives. Therefore, don't worry, and instead trust God. Take him at his word and believe in his provision for you.

Reflection Questions

1. What do you worry about most?

2. How does trusting God for our basic needs bring perspective to our worries?

Prayer

Father, you created the whole earth and everything in it. You gave the first man a garden to enjoy, relationships, and food. While he spurned this gift (and we do too), we trust that in your love and grace you will continue to provide for our most basic needs. Help us, Lord, to give our anxieties over to you. Let us worry less and break us free from the marketing that deceives us into thinking we need more. Give us satisfaction in our daily bread alone, and let us give thanks for it. Amen.

DAY 95

Q. What do we pray for in the seventh and eighth lines
of the Lord's Prayer?

A. In the seventh and eighth lines of the Lord's Prayer,
we pray that God would forgive our sins by looking to
Jesus Christ and that we might forgive others as
Christ forgave us.

And forgive us our debts, as we also have forgiven our debtors.

—MATTHEW 6:12

OUR DEFAULT RESPONSE TO the evil in the world around us is vengeance.
We mask our desire for vengeance in language that makes it all very legal and sophisticated. We hear things such as "we want justice," but this
is merely thinly veiled language intended to disguise our real desire for
vengeance. "This person hurt me and now I want them to pay for it" really means "I want that person to experience hurt, equal to or greater than
the hurt perpetrated against me." Vengeance is our default response to evil,
and in the name of "justice" atrocities have been carried out for thousands
and thousands of years by people groups, political institutions, nations, and
individuals. This is why the biblical ethic of forgiving grace is such a radical
concept. It flies in the face of our most basic human desire for vengeance,
for retribution.

Ironically, our desire for justice condemns each and every one of us
before God. We all long for the world to be made right and desire a perfectly just world, but we ourselves perpetuate injustices and sin against God
in innumerable ways, ways we may not even fully understand because our

197

hearts deceive us. We might think we are acting towards a just cause, but in many cases these causes are radically opposed to the way of Jesus, and thus act to create further injustice in the world. A good example of this is the growing political divide in the West. It seems that more people are aligning themselves with political organizations such as Antifa, The Proud Boys, and race-related groups which actively participate in violence and vitriolic rhetoric, furthering injustice instead of ending it. True justice has never come from unjust means. Unjust means only further entrenches injustice, exacerbating the human desire for vengeance. This is only one example—and perhaps a controversial one—of how our hearts deceive us and lead us into sin.

This is why it was necessary that God the Son, in his love, came in the person of Jesus Christ. He gave himself over to the injustices of the world so that our sin might be paid for by him on the cross. His death made forgiveness a possibility because he, independent of our works, paid the penalty for our sinfulness and forgives our sin. Now when we come to God in prayer, we can ask him for forgiveness and receive it because of Christ's great work. When we come to God asking for forgiveness, we are made righteous through Christ and filled with the Holy Spirit who enables us to walk in a newness of life. This sets us on a path away from injustices and towards true justice.

Yet, the Lord's Prayer does not simply say God forgives us, but it also reminds us that God's forgiveness is to be extended towards other people through us. His unmerited grace towards us is to be reflected in our lives as we deal with other people. We are not called to seek vengeance, but rather to love those who harm us. This principle is shown to us in the famous phrase "turn the other cheek." Jesus says, "Do not resist an evil person. If anyone slaps you on the right cheek, turn to them the other cheek also" (Matt 5:39). Nonviolent resistance in the face of evil is perhaps the most countercultural teaching of Scripture today.

Reflection Questions

1. What injustices make you extremely angry with the world and other people?

2. Are you seeking to forgive those people, or are you seeking vengeance?

Day 95

Prayer

Lord Jesus, thank you for the work of the cross, where you paid the price for our sins and demonstrated your forgiving love. Teach us to forgive by your Holy Spirit and forgive us for our unwillingness to forgive. Search our hearts and show us where we are bitter against our brothers and sisters. Let us bring our grievances to light and seek forgiveness. Amen.

Day 96

Q. What do we pray for in final lines of the Lord's Prayer?

A. In the final lines of the Lord's Prayer, we pray that God would protect us when we are facing temptations so that we might not sin.

And lead us not into temptation, but deliver us from the evil one.

—MATTHEW 6:13

FOR A LOT OF people, it's harder to believe in the existence of evil spirits than it is to believe in God. Belief in demons and evil spirits is viewed as being born out of old-school superstition. They are viewed as remnants of a bygone stale worldview that doesn't take science seriously. It's antiquated and downright silly to even suggest such things are real.

Yet when we look at Scripture it is crystal-clear about the existence of evil forces in the world. There is no doubt that the apostle Paul thought these beings were real: "For our struggle is not against flesh and blood, but against the rulers, against the authorities, against the powers of this dark world and against the spiritual forces of evil in the heavenly realms" (Eph 6:12). Even Jesus acknowledged their reality as he talked with evil spirits, cast them out, and ruled over them during his earthly ministry. Thus, to deny their reality would be to presume that the biblical witness is incorrect. Indeed, it would be to say the Son of God was incorrect.

Since these beings are real, the Lord's Prayer ends with a request asking for protection from evil forces. First, we ask the Lord to lead us by his Holy Spirit away from temptation, whether that temptation is coming from an external force, such as an evil spirit, or is coming from within us, because of our own sinful desires. In either case, we can be sure God will not allow us to be tempted beyond what we can handle (1 Cor 10:13). Despite the presence of evil in our own hearts and the presence of evil in the world around us, God is still in control. He guides us so that we can walk in step with him. Secondly, we ask the Lord to protect us from the evil one, Satan, which we can be certain he will do. We know that God has dealt a fatal blow to the forces of evil with the power of the cross and Jesus' resurrection. We also know that a day will come when Satan will be defeated and destroyed once and for all. Since both of these realities are true, we can have confidence that the Lord will guard us from the evil one and lead us away from temptation as we come to him in prayer.

Reflection Questions

1. What comes to mind when we ask God to deliver us from the evil one?

2. Why is it hard to take seriously the Scriptures' warnings regarding evil spirits?

Prayer

Father, you are sovereign over all things. You are even sovereign over the forces of evil in this world, and you alone have defeated them with the cross. Lord thank you for the gift of the cross and your Son Jesus. Amen.

DAY 97

Q. What does the biblical story teach us about creation?

A. The biblical story teaches us that God created
the world good.

But ask the animals, and they will teach you, or the birds in the sky, and they will tell you; or speak to the earth, and it will teach you, or let the fish in the sea inform you. Which of all these does not know that the hand of the Lord has done this? In his hand is the life of every creature and the breath of all mankind.

—JOB 12:7-10

AS WE READ THE Bible, we are confronted with a story. Scripture has a narrative arc that extends through all its sixty-six books, finding its completion in Revelation. While this story has not yet been finished in actual history, we know that God is working towards accomplishing his purposes and bringing it to an end. We know that one day Jesus Christ will return to set all things right in the universe and when he does there will be no more pain, tears, mourning, or anything evil (Rev 21:1–4). As believers in Jesus, we can have confidence that this will be accomplished because 1) God has promised it and has always been faithful in fulfilling his promises, and 2) because the Holy Spirit testifies to this in our hearts as we trust in Christ.

The next four questions-and-answers—including this one—elaborate on the plot of God's grand narrative. Specifically, they discuss the central markers of that plot through the terms of creation, fall, redemption, and salvation. Through these plot-markers we see the fullness of the gospel, or the good news, of Jesus Christ. Therefore, we will briefly examine each of these markers, recapping some of the things we have discussed in previous questions-and-answers. Yet this is not a bad thing. Repetition is the beginning of learning. If you are reading this and do not fully remember the other questions-and-answers these plot-markers will aid you immensely.

Our first plot-marker is creation. Here we are reminded that God is the Creator of the entire universe. As we have seen earlier, God spoke the universe into existence (Gen 1:3). This does not only show us that he is a Creator—technically he could create the universe while being some semi-divine underling—but it shows us that he is all-powerful, what theologians call omnipotence. He isn't a divine subordinate, but the Alpha and Omega. After God had spoken the world into existence, he declared that everything he made "was very good" (Gen 1:31). Now goodness is a relative concept to us. We think of *good* as something we enjoy or like, something that is not bad. However, here *good* means *perfect*. God created the universe in such a way that it was exactly how he wanted it to be. It was free from all defects and, in particular, it was free from human sinfulness.

God placed Adam and Eve, the first people, in this perfect world. Their job was to tend to creation, to care for it, and to rule over it. They were meant to be, more or less, little "g" gods for the world. They would rule with justice, caring for the earth so that all of creation flourished. Most importantly, God actually dwelt with them as they accomplished this task. It wasn't just that they had all the outward trappings of a perfect life, they also had perfect fellowship with each other and God. Their relationships were free from evil. No lying, no backstabbing, no mean words, just sheer perfection.

This was the way God intended the world to be by his will of desire. He wanted the world to be a perfect place of fellowship with God, other people, and nature. In short, it was paradise on earth. Unfortunately, as we know from the way the world is now, things did not stay this way. What happened? Well, that is the subject of our next question-and-answer.

Reflection Questions

1. What does it mean that the Bible has a narrative arc?

2. What images come to mind when you think of the way God intended the creation to be?

DAY 97

Prayer

Heavenly Father, you are the all-powerful Creator of the universe. You didn't just create everything, but you made it good. You made it just the way you wanted it. Lord, we long for this. We long for the day when all things will be made right. Help us to look to Jesus and trust that he will return to accomplish this task. Amen.

DAY 98

Q. What does the biblical story teach us about the fall?

A. The biblical story teaches us that people fell into sin.

You come to the help of those who gladly do right, who remember your ways. But when we continued to sin against them, you were angry. How then can we be saved? All of us have become like one who is unclean, and all our righteous acts are like filthy rags; we all shrivel up like a leaf, and like the wind our sins sweep us away. No one calls on your name or strives to lay hold of you; for you have hidden your face from us and have given us over to our sins.

—ISAIAH 64:5–7

THE REALITY OF THE world is much harsher than the world that we read about in Genesis 1 and 2. When we hear that God created all things good, and that everyone was happy in his creation, we immediately think, "What happened?" The answer to that question is the next plot-marker in the biblical story: it is the event that Christians call *the fall*.

After God created everything good and perfect, he gave Adam and Eve one command: they were not to eat from the tree of good and evil (Gen 2:17). It's important for us to note here that God did not place some sort of magical tree in the garden, but rather this tree which God told them to avoid represented the knowledge of God. For them to eat from this tree would be to strive after God's knowledge. To eat from the tree, would mean they didn't accept God's perfect will for their lives. It would mean they wanted to rule over the creation, independent of its Creator. If they ate from its fruit, they were essentially admitting that their hearts had turned from a place of worship to a desire for domination.

In Genesis 3, this is exactly what we see happen. Adam and Eve eat from the tree, demonstrating that their hearts have been deceived into thinking they do not need God. As a result of this horrible error in judgment, the relationship that people had with God, with each other, and with nature, was severed. The entirety of humanity was now marred by sin. All of humanity became disobedient to God. Due to this, the world has, from that moment on, seen radical acts of violence, the exploitation of nature, fractures in human relationships, and so much more. The fall is the reason for genocide, it's the reason for divorce, it's the reason for abuse, it's the reason behind the climate crisis, it's the reason for every act of evil in the world.

Furthermore, because the first people sinned and essentially broke the world, we also sin. We contribute to the brokenness of the world because we exist in a world that has experienced the fall. But God, even though he had a full right to destroy humanity in his wrath and start over, didn't. Instead, he began working in the lives of particular people to provide a path for restoration. He, in his grace, set out to accomplish a plan, a rescue mission to save humanity. This rescue mission is the subject of the next plot-marker in our questions-and-answers.

Reflection Questions

1. What did the tree of the knowledge of good and evil represent for the first human beings?

2. How do you see the world as a broken place? What sins do you notice most?

Prayer

Holy and wonderful Father, forgive us for our sin. We have sinned just like Adam and Eve. We continue to sin each and every day. Apart from your grace we are completely lost. Father, we put our hope in Jesus Christ, who made it so that our sins can be forgiven. Let us trust in this forgiveness today we pray. Amen.

DAY 99

Q. What does the biblical story teach us about redemption?

A. The biblical story teaches us that God sent his Son to save people from sin.

Therefore, if anyone is in Christ, the new creation has come: The old has gone, the new is here! All this is from God, who reconciled us to himself through Christ and gave us the ministry of reconciliation: that God was reconciling the world to himself in Christ, not counting people's sins against them. And he has committed to us the message of reconciliation. We are therefore Christ's ambassadors, as though God were making his appeal through us. We implore you on Christ's behalf: Be reconciled to God. God made him who had no sin to be sin for us, so that in him we might become the righteousness of God.

—2 CORINTHIANS 5:17-21

As CHRISTIANS WE PUT our hope in the person that this particular plot-marker refers to. Now that he has come, we no longer live under the old order of brokenness. Yet, at the same time, we continue to experience brokenness as we wait patiently for the full restoration of all things. We live in the tension of the already-not-yet kingdom of God.

This kingdom was ushered in through the work of God's Son, Jesus Christ. It is through him and in him that we find our hope and salvation. As we discussed in our last question-and-answer all people, without exception, have given in to their sinful desires and are deserving of God's judgment. Even if, hypothetically, someone never committed a sinful action—they never broke one of God's laws—they would still deserve the punishment of God. The reason being that this person would not have acted righteously, they would have only completed what was required of them. As we learn from Luke's Gospel, "Will he thank the servant because he did what he was told to do?" (Luke 17:9). Therefore, even if we could fully obey God's law, we would still deserve God's wrath because our sinful nature still remains. We would have only fulfilled our duties to God. We still would not be able to earn his favor.

It appears then that humanity is in a dire situation. Apart from the express work of God it would be impossible for humanity to find salvation. Nothing we do could ever earn our way up to heaven. Nothing we do could ever earn God's favor. The debt owed because of our crimes is infinite in scope, not because our crimes are infinite, but because God is infinite. The only way for humanity to be saved is if something, or rather someone, of infinite value paid the infinite legal debt we owed. Thus, God sent his Son, Jesus Christ, who was fully God and fully man, to pay this debt with his life. This great exchange, the life of the God-man for us, is what we call redemption.

Before we move on, however, it is important that we understand what is meant by the word *sent* in the context of our question-and-answer. It is not as if God sent a lesser being than himself. Likewise, it isn't entirely true that God the Father sent himself. Rather, the Son was sent in the sense that the Godhead—Father, Son, and Holy Spirit—with one will, sent him for this purpose. God did not send an unwilling participant, but rather Father, Son, and Holy Spirit, with one will, enacted this plan of redemption.

This is good news. It means that God has made a way for us to be reconciled to him by the blood of his Son. It means God has, in effect, reversed the effects of the fall through Jesus' blood. If we come to accept this atoning sacrifice, believing that Jesus was God the Son incarnate, then we have our sins forgiven and we are given the righteousness of Christ as a free gift. We are indwelt by the Holy Spirit and empowered with the newness of life that comes from being made righteous. This is what makes God's plan of redemption so glorious. Yet, despite its glory, it is not God's final act.

Reflection Questions

1. Why did Jesus, fully God and fully man, have to die for our sins to be forgiven?

2. What does it mean that God *sent* the Son? Was he an unwilling participant?

Prayer

Gracious God, we thank you for the glorious plan of redemption you decreed from eternity past with one will as Father, Son, and Holy Spirit. Father, thank you for sending your Son to die so that our sins might be forgiven. Jesus, thank you for sending the Holy Spirit to lead us into all truth. Holy Spirit, thank you for illuminating our hearts to see this great plan of redemption. Lord, help us to know and love you more each and every day. Amen.

Day 100

Q. What does the biblical story teach us about restoration?

A. The biblical story teaches us that Jesus will return to restore all things to perfection.

See, I will create new heavens and a new earth. The former things will not be remembered, nor will they come to mind. But be glad and rejoice forever in what I will create, for I will create Jerusalem to be a delight and its people a joy. I will rejoice over Jerusalem and take delight in my people; the sound of weeping and of crying will be heard in it no more.

—ISAIAH 65:17–19

THE FINAL ACT OF the biblical story is yet to be accomplished. We are eagerly waiting for this final act to occur because it marks the end of all sorrow, all tears, all violence, all sin. In redemption, Jesus paid the debt we owed to God for our sin on the cross. His first coming demonstrated his lordship and inaugurated his in-breaking kingdom. Yet, the fullness of the kingdom has not yet come. Sin and brokenness still exist and still deeply effect our lives.

But once the fullness of time is complete, and God has finished patiently enduring with the vessels of wrath, Jesus Christ will return to make all things new. Jesus will come and there will be a final resurrection of the dead where everyone who ever lived will be judged. Some will be judged according to the grace of God as evidenced by their belief in Jesus Christ, while others will be judged according to their evil works. Those who have believed will inherit eternal life, and those who have not will inherit eternal punishment (Matt 25:31–46).

Finally, all things will be made new. There will be a great restoration of everything to the perfection enjoyed before the fall of Adam and Eve. God himself will enter into this new creation and dwell with his people there for all eternity. He will be their comfort, their joy, and their source of peace in the new creation. There will be no more hunger, war, crime, or death. Everything will be perfected for those who put their trust in Jesus Christ.

This is not a cyclical story. It is not as if God created all things good, we fell, he sent his Son to die, and restored everything back to the way it was in the garden so that it could all happen again. It doesn't come full circle and risk repeating itself *ad infinitum*. No, rather the biblical story is linear. It begins with creation and ends with *new* creation. It begins with a garden and ends with the city of God. Even if Adam and Eve had lived the perfect life they still would have been moving on a forward trajectory towards the revealing of God's Son, the indwelling of the Holy Spirit, and the perfected city of God. Yet, to ponder such hypotheticals is pointless.

Simply put, when we turn to Scripture—as we read it from Genesis to Revelation—we see one single narrative arc the whole way through. We see humanity created to dwell in a near-perfect world, we see them fall from their innocence into sin, we see humankind wrestling with the reality of sin through history, we see God's promise of redemption, we see his fulfillment of those promises in Jesus Christ, and we see the longing in patience for the new creation where all things will be made perfect, where heaven and earth will be united together as one, where God will talk with us face to face and we will forever behold his glory.

Reflection Questions

3. What do you most look forward to about the restoration of all things?

4. Have these plot-markers shifted your view of Scripture at all?

Prayer

Holy Father, thank you so much for you word. We are so deeply indebted to you and we are eternally thankful for the gracious gifts you bestow upon us. Help us to know you in a deeper and more meaningful way each and every day. Let us trust in you completely for our salvation and show us your Son, Jesus Christ, through the Holy Spirit. Amen.

Epilogue

A FOUNDATION IS NOT meant to stand alone. Imagine if a developer set out to rezone an entire neighborhood, purchased all the lots, got his construction crew to start work, completed the foundations, and then simply left the project half-done. Imagine further that he were to claim that the work had been completed and attempted to sell these lots of "fully-formed foundations." Certainly, people would think this developer was out of his mind. Who wants a measly foundation with no home upon it? Who wants a shelter with no walls, no roof, no bathroom? No one! To simply pretend, as the developer did, that the homes were complete when all that had been done was the laying of a foundation is pure lunacy. Similarly, for us to pretend our journey into biblical study, theological study, and the Christian faith is complete with the reading of this book is equally mad.

This book was written as a foundation of sorts. Its purpose was to give the reader basic categories for further study, reflection, prayer, and thought. It is meant to be merely the beginning of a journey, not the end. It is a foundation and it's not meant to stand alone. Therefore, let me admonish you to continue that journey. Continue to explore the Christian faith and continue to build upon this foundation. There is so much more work to be done. So much so that you could spend a lifetime building upon these foundational elements. So, build, and build well. Yet, how can this be accomplished? How should you build upon this foundation? Let me suggest some ways that you can add walls, a roof, and all the other accoutrements of a beautiful home: biblical study, theological study, prayer, and community.

The first way I would like to suggest you continue to build upon this foundation is through the continual study of God's word, Scripture. Whether this book has been utilized as a curriculum in a church or read as a personal devotional text, let me encourage you to continue reading Scripture beyond this work. The greatest movements of renewal in the church have always begun with a renewed desire to read the Bible. The

Reformation of the fifteenth century was started through Martin Luther's study of the book of Romans. The early church turned to the Old Testament Scriptures to argue for the truth of Jesus Christ. Perhaps in our own day, as people commit in a fresh way to study the Bible, we will experience a renewal of thought similar to other great movements in history. Set yourself up with a Bible-reading plan and utilize it every day. Make use of a study Bible, an invaluable tool for the novice of biblical studies. Listen to textually based sermons on your way to work or as you finish chores. There are a multitude of ways you can get into God's word consistently, and as we do, we build upon the foundation we have laid.

Secondly, engage in theological study. Unfortunately, in my experience, there is a growing anti-intellectualism in the Western church. Rigorous academic study and utilizing the potential of human reason to grow deeper in our knowledge of God is seen as opposed to the ways of the Holy Spirit. The power of the Holy Spirit is seen as being more of a felt experience than an intellectual motivator. This is patently false and extremely dangerous. God designed the human intellect, he created it and molded it, so that it might glorify him in everything. The intellect is not a threat to knowing God, it is an aid in knowing God. Thus, we should utilize it. We should cast off the idea that an intellectually rigorous faith is somehow inauthentic. Rather let us use our minds to their full potential for the glory of God. Study the ancient creeds,* follow teachers who care about what they are expositing, examine the history of the church, and read challenging books. Read Herman Bavinck, John Calvin, Martin Luther, Anselm, and Augustine. Read contemporary authors such as R. C. Sproul, Tim Keller, and the late J. I. Packer. Enjoy the rich theological tradition of the protestant church and, as you engage in it, be built up.

Thirdly, spend time in prayer every single day. God has spoken to us in his word—engage with it, learn from it, and then pray through it. Come to God and bring your requests before him. Speak with him as you take up his word for you. Ask him to grow you, help you, and remind you of his love. Confess your sins to him and repent. Thank him for everything he has accomplished in your life. Prayer is the personal communion we have with God. It's a gift of his grace to us as a result of the work of Jesus Christ on our behalf. He hears us as his own sons and daughters. We should enjoy this gift and come to God with boldness, knowing he hears us and blesses us as

*You can find some of the ancient creeds in the Appendix.

we pray. Think of prayer as the food which powers the laborers to continue building upon the foundation, to raise the walls and put up the roof.

The final thing necessary for our growth as Christians is community, specifically the community that is found within the local church. We cannot grow apart from faithful brothers and sisters in Christ. We need them to rebuke us when we sin. To pray for us when we are weak. To worship with us and encourage us with their love. Yet, the church is not merely an institution existing for the individual believer's benefit. It is also God's chosen instrument to bring the gospel to a dying world. The church is the place where the poor are truly loved, materially and spiritually. The church is where people find healing for their souls. The church is where God's word is spoken. The church is where true reconciliation can take place between warring factions, races, and other groups. We need the church. So, find a local church which preaches the gospel from the Bible, believes in the historic creeds, and has a desire to see more people come to saving faith in Jesus Christ. I sincerely believe that, if we wish to build upon the foundation this book has attempted to provide, then we must engage in biblical study, theological study, prayer, and join a local community of believers.

While this book claims to lay a foundation for faith it is important that we remember the cornerstone of this foundation, Jesus Christ. Apart from Jesus Christ our faith is an impossibility. It is only through him that we are saved from our deepest, most pernicious problem, sin. His death has appeased God's wrath towards sin and secured his favor towards us. His resurrection has provided the possibility for new life and we long for the day when we too will inherit resurrection bodies. His sending of the Holy Spirit to illuminate us, regenerate us, and indwell us makes Christ's presence known to us. He transforms our hearts and gives us new affections and desires so that we might love God and others. And one day he will return to set all things right, once and for all. This book is nothing more than an attempt to honor Jesus Christ, the cornerstone of all solid foundations, I pray it has accomplished this task.

Consequently, you are no longer foreigners and strangers, but fellow citizens with God's people and also members of his household, built on the foundation of the apostles and prophets, with Christ Jesus himself as the chief cornerstone. In him the whole building is joined together and rises to become a holy temple in the Lord. And in him you too are being built together to become a dwelling in which God lives by his Spirit.

—EPHESIANS 2:19–22

Appendix

The Apostles' Creed

I believe in God, the Father almighty,
creator of heaven and earth.
I believe in Jesus Christ, his only Son, our Lord.
He was conceived by the power of the Holy Spirit
and born of the Virgin Mary.
He suffered under Pontius Pilate,
was crucified, died, and was buried.
He descended to the dead.
On the third day he rose again.
He ascended into heaven,
and is seated at the right hand of the Father.
He will come again to judge the living and the dead.
I believe in the Holy Spirit,
the holy catholic Church,
the communion of saints,
the forgiveness of sins,
the resurrection of the body,
and the life everlasting. Amen.

The Nicene Creed

I believe in one God, the Father Almighty, Maker of heaven and earth, and
of all things visible and invisible.

And in one Lord Jesus Christ, the only begotten Son of God, begotten of
the Father before all worlds; God of God, Light of Light, very God of very

God; begotten, not made, being of one substance with the Father by whom all things were made.

Who, for us men and for our salvation, came down from heaven, and was incarnate by the Holy Spirit of the virgin Mary, and was made man; and was crucified also for us under Pontius Pilate; He suffered and was buried; and the third day He rose again, according to the Scriptures; and ascended into heaven, and sitteth on the right hand of the Father; and He shall come again, with glory, to judge the living and the dead; whose kingdom shall have no end.

And I believe in the Holy Spirit, the Lord and Giver of life; who proceedeth from the Father and the Son; who with the Father and the Son together is worshipped and glorified; who spoke by the prophets.

And I believe in one holy catholic and apostolic church. I acknowledge one baptism for the remission of sins; and I look for the resurrection of the dead, and the life of the world to come.

Amen

Chalcedonian Creed

We, then, following the holy fathers, all with one consent teach men to confess one and the same Son, our Lord Jesus Christ, the same perfect in Godhead and also perfect in manhood; truly God and truly man, of a rational soul and body; coessential with the Father according to the Godhead, and consubstantial with us according to the manhood; in all things like unto us, without sin; begotten before all ages of the Father according to the Godhead, and in these latter days, for us and for our salvation, born of the Virgin Mary, the mother of God, according to the manhood; one and the same Christ, Son, Lord, Only begotten, to be acknowledged in two natures, without confusion, without change, without division, without separation; the distinction of natures being by no means taken away by the union, but rather the property of each nature being preserved, and concurring in one person and one subsistence, not parted or divided into two persons, but one and the same Son, and only begotten, God the Word, the Lord Jesus Christ; as the prophets from the beginning have declared concerning Him, and the Lord Jesus Christ Himself has taught us, and the creed of the holy fathers has handed down to us.

Bibliography

Augustine. *The Confessions*. Chicago: Moody, 2007.

Bird, Michael F. *What Christians Ought to Believe: An Introduction to Christian Doctrine through the Apostles' Creed*. Grand Rapids: Zondervan Academic, 2016.

Bloesch, Donald. *The Church: Sacraments, Worship, Ministry, Mission*. Downers Grove, IL: InterVarsity, 2002.

————. *Holy Scripture: Revelation, Inspiration, and Interpretation*. Downers Grove, IL: InterVarsity, 1994.

Bonhoeffer, Dietrich. *Ethics*. Minneapolis: Fortress, 2015.

Brakel, Wilhelmus à. *The Christian's Reasonable Service, Volume 1: God, Man, and Christ*. 4 vols. Grand Rapids: Reformation Heritage, 2020.

Dean, Kenda Creasy. *Almost Christian: What the Faith of Our Teenagers Is Telling the American Church*. New York: Oxford University Press, 2010.

Melville, Herman. *Moby Dick*. London: Arcturus, 2019.

Smith, James K.A. *On the Road with Saint Augustine: A Real-World Spirituality for Restless Hearts*. Grand Rapids: Brazos, 2019.

Solzhenitsyn, Aleksandr. *The Gulag Archipelago: The Authorized Abridgement*. New York: Harper Perennial, 2007.

Westminster Assembly. "The Westminster Shorter Catechism." https://prts.edu/wp-content/uploads/2013/09/Shorter_Catechism.pdf.

CPSIA information can be obtained
at www.ICGtesting.com
Printed in the USA
BVHW040721170921
616730BV00043B/62